500
——
1d

THOMAS R. ATKINSON
WITH THE ASSISTANCE OF
ELIZABETH T. SIMPSON

TRENDS IN CORPORATE BOND QUALITY

STUDIES IN
CORPORATE BOND FINANCING
NUMBER 4

NATIONAL BUREAU OF ECONOMIC RESEARCH
NEW YORK 1967
Distributed by COLUMBIA UNIVERSITY PRESS
NEW YORK AND LONDON

RELATION OF THE DIRECTORS TO THE WORK AND PUBLICATIONS OF THE NATIONAL BUREAU OF ECONOMIC RESEARCH

1. The object of the National Bureau of Economic Research is to ascertain and to present to the public important economic facts and their interpretation in a scientific and impartial manner. The Board of Directors is charged with the responsibility of ensuring that the work of the National Bureau is carried on in strict conformity with this object.
2. To this end the Board of Directors shall appoint one or more Directors of Research.
3. The Director or Directors of Research shall submit to the members of the Board, or to its Executive Committee, for their formal adoption, all specific proposals concerning researches to be instituted.
4. No report shall be published until the Director or Directors of Research shall have submitted to the Board a summary drawing attention to the character of the data and their utilization in the report, the nature and treatment of the problems involved, the main conclusions, and such other information as in their opinion would serve to determine the suitability of the report for publication in accordance with the principles of the National Bureau.
5. A copy of any manuscript proposed for publication shall also be submitted to each member of the Board. For each manuscript to be so submitted a special committee shall be appointed by the President, or at his designation by the Executive Director, consisting of three Directors selected as nearly as may be one from each general division of the Board. The names of the special manuscript committee shall be stated to each Director when the summary and report described in paragraph (4) are sent to him. It shall be the duty of each member of the committee to read the manuscript. If each member of the special committee signifies his approval within thirty days, the manuscript may be published. If each member of the special committee has not signified his approval within thirty days of the transmittal of the report and manuscript, the Director of Research shall then notify each member of the Board, requesting approval or disapproval of publication, and thirty additional days shall be granted for this purpose. The manuscript shall then not be published unless at least a majority of the entire Board and a two-thirds majority of those members of the Board who shall have voted on the proposal within the time fixed for the receipt of votes on the publication proposed shall have approved.
6. No manuscript may be published, though approved by each member of the special committee, until forty-five days have elapsed from the transmittal of the summary and report. The interval is allowed for the receipt of any memorandum of dissent or reservation, together with a brief statement of his reasons, that any member may wish to express; and such memorandum of dissent or reservation shall be published with the manuscript if he so desires. Publication does not, however, imply that each member of the Board has read the manuscript, or that either members of the Board in general, or of the special committee, have passed upon its validity in every detail.
7. A copy of this resolution shall, unless otherwise determined by the Board, be printed in each copy of every National Bureau book.

(Resolution adopted October 25, 1926,
as revised February 6, 1933, and February 24, 1941)

The high level of investor confidence since World War II, and the large and expanding volume of bond financing, raise important questions as to the quality of bond credit in the postwar period. Although our records do not cover this period—and even if they did, a retrospective test of quality could not be undertaken until the market had been subjected to a real test—the record of the past is sufficiently strong to suggest the need for constant review of bond market standards.

W. BRADDOCK HICKMAN, *Corporate Bond Quality and Investor Experience,* 1958

CONTENTS

TABLES

CHARTS

ACKNOWLEDGMENTS

Pressure of other duties at crucial times caused me to rely to a great extent upon Elizabeth Simpson of the National Bureau's staff, and her help has indeed been invaluable. Not only had Miss Simpson been an important member of the earlier corporate bond project but her versatility and her willingness to look at the subject again in the light of new conditions made the difference between success and failure.

I have incurred debts to many others in the compilation of this report. James S. Earley, Geoffrey H. Moore, Avery B. Cohan, and Roger F. Murray made useful criticisms of earlier drafts. I am grateful for advice on difficult points from Norman Michigan of the National Association of Insurance Commissioners, Sidney Homer of Salomon Brothers & Hutzler, and Herman Liss of Scudder, Stevens & Clark. James J. O'Leary and Robert H. Parks, Life Insurance Association of America, and Orson Hart, New York Life Insurance Company, gave me helpful advice. The directors' reading committee of the National Bureau, consisting of Robert V. Roosa, Frank W. Fetter, and Donald B. Woodward, finally, played their part in reviewing the study. An additional helpful suggestion was made by Director Vincent W. Bladen.

Susan Sheehan did the initial task of compiling the basic statistics, although updating was done by several others. Anne Burgess, Ruth Heisler, and Esther Chan were of much assistance with other tasks dealing with the manuscript. Joan Tron edited the MS. and H. Irving Forman drew the charts; I gratefully acknowledge their skill.

Finally, to my wife and children I owe a note of gratitude for their forbearance.

T. R. A.

January 1966

FOREWORD

Atkinson's study of postwar corporate bonds in the United States is the third report on the business sector to appear in the National Bureau's program of studies in the quality of credit. Albert Wojnilower's *The Quality of Bank Loans* (1962) and Martin Seiden's *The Quality of Trade Credit* (1964) covered the other two major elements of the debt of American business enterprise. Since trade credit, commercial bank loans, and bonded debt constitute the overwhelming proportion of business indebtedness, Atkinson's study rounds out the program's coverage of the business sector. The program has been supported in large part by a grant from the Merrill Foundation for Advancement of Financial Knowledge, Inc.

To the degree that was possible, this study represents an updating of W. Braddock Hickman's volume, *Corporate Bond Quality and Investor Experience*.[1] That Atkinson's study is of moderate length is not because of any decline in the importance of bonds as a source of American business finance. As he shows, corporate bonds have remained a major source of business funds since the war. Two other factors are instead responsible.

First, the resources available for this postwar study were small compared with those devoted to the National Bureau's corporate bond project, on which the Hickman studies rested. Second, the postwar performance of corporate bonds has been so strong that the detailed statistical examination of the relations between the characteristics of bonds and their performance, which comprised a large part of Hickman's study, was not feasible for the postwar period.

Indeed, the postwar years have been so free of bond defaults that one might conclude that no quality problem exists. However, the Hickman study supplies a warning. One of its salient findings was that investor confidence engendered by extended periods of prosperity appears to generate security issues of less than prime quality. Atkinson

[1] Princeton University Press for National Bureau of Economic Research, 1958.

carefully examines the characteristics of postwar bond issues for evidence of such changing "ex ante" quality, covering all of the important variables that Hickman employed.

Atkinson supplements the earlier study in another important respect. Hickman studied bonds in an era when the bulk of them were "public offerings," whereas in the postwar years the placement of securities by direct negotiation between borrower and investor has become of almost equal importance. In the case of industrials, the direct placement (along with its half-sister, the commercial bank term loan) has become the dominant form of corporate long-term financing. By examining the records of the National Association of Insurance Commissioners, which rates a large share of direct placements, and by using the new information gathered by Avery Cohan on the direct placements of life insurance companies, Atkinson has been able to make some judgments regarding the quality of this increasingly important share of corporate debt.[2]

Hickman included bonds convertible into stock in his study, but did not analyze the influence of this feature on default or market performance. In view of the fact that in postwar years the share of publicly offered bonds containing the convertibility feature has been more substantial than before the war, Atkinson gives specific attention to such securities. Upon re-examining the Hickman data, he found that default experience in prewar periods was considerably poorer for convertible issues than for nonconvertibles. He appraises the prevalence of the convertibility feature in postwar corporate bond issues in the light of this finding.

In these several important respects, therefore, the present study augments our knowledge of the quality characteristics of business debt and its record of performance.

JAMES S. EARLEY, Director
Quality of Credit Studies

[2] Cohan's own study of the yields and quality of direct placements, undertaken as part of the National Bureau's interest rate study, is in progress.

INTRODUCTION AND SUMMARY

What has happened to the quality of corporate bonds in the period since the end of World War II? Has the risk in investing in these bonds increased or lessened from the early postwar period to recent years? How does their potential exposure to default and loss compare now with the period of the 1920's? In these pages various facets of quality are examined, following with some variation the tests developed by W. Braddock Hickman in *Corporate Bond Quality and Investor Experience* [1] for the 1900–43 period.

Whereas Hickman's material was compiled from a thorough search of all records of bond offerings plus year-by-year examination of the financial statements of major American corporations, this study principally drew upon investment service listings of public offerings and a separate compilation of announcements of bond issues to be placed directly with the ultimate holder (direct placements). Some findings of other authors, including the excellent sample of direct placements compiled by Avery Cohan for the period from 1951 through 1961, were also utilized. [2] Defaults were studied by compiling lists from the investment manuals as well as lists of corporations undergoing reorganization under Chapter X of the Bankruptcy Act. Finally, to cover some points not explicitly covered by Hickman, special tabulations were made of the data for the earlier period, particularly the 1920's.

Two related qualifications of the present study should be noted. First, in the absence of a major depression in the postwar period one cannot be sure that measurements of selected characteristics and tabulation of an admittedly minimal number of defaults give a true indication of how safe (or risky) the current increase of corporate bonds is, particularly relative to previous bond issues that experienced a severe economic test. Of course, it may be argued that with some advance in

---

[1] Princeton University Press for National Bureau of Economic Research, 1958.

[2] Further analysis of the quality characteristics of direct placements is expected to issue from Cohan's study, which is a part of the National Bureau's interest rate project.

economic knowledge and a greater degree of recognition of governmental responsibility for determining the course of the economy, recessions in the future may be limited to roughly the amplitude and duration of those experienced since World War II. Lacking here any conclusive proof on this point, the reader should interpret the findings on bond quality in the light of his own views about the likelihood that recent recessions will be typical of the severity of the economic test that the future will hold.

Second, in the absence of a substantial volume of actual defaults (because, apparently, they did not occur), most of the analysis is based upon so-called ex ante indicators of corporate bond quality, that is, the presence or absence of characteristics found to have been associated with default and loss in previous periods (for the most part, the 1900–43 period studied by Hickman). In this sense the postwar study of bond quality seeks to measure risk exposure to a given situation rather than to determine how many bonds currently outstanding can be expected to go bad over their lifetime. That the data are less than perfect for this task is obvious. On the other hand, standards of judgment of bond quality have not gone through the revolution that has characterized mortgage lending or consumer lending terms, nor have corporate bonds shown the proliferation of forms that has generally characterized bank loans to business. Indeed, the most conspicuous change, that of the development of serial payment for direct placements, is thought by some to be reassuring. While direct placements and convertibles have played important roles in the corporate bond field in the postwar period, these forms of obligation have existed for many years. Standards for maturity and earnings coverage have been fixed for many years also. Because no vast changes in corporate bond characteristics have occurred, ex ante characteristics, that is, those previously found to be associated with actual casualties, should not be misleading.

These are the findings of the study:

1. U.S. corporate bonds defaulting in the postwar period (from 1945 through 1965) averaged less than 0.1 per cent of the volume outstanding, or about one-half billion dollars in all. This compares with 1.7 per cent of the outstanding bonds which defaulted during 1900–43. The postwar defaults were concentrated in bonds of the railroad industry, many of which had been outstanding before 1920 or had been refundings of original bonds issued prior to that year.

2. Defaults in the postwar period were not concentrated in a particular cycle phase, perhaps because recessions were not severe. Bonds issued in the postwar period and defaulting from 1944 to 1965 were, however, largely offered in years of business peaks or one year before the cycle peak. From these facts we conclude that although bond defaults have not been a significant problem in the postwar period, the process whereby bonds are offered and some subsequently default continues to be associated with business cycles.

3. Direct placements in the postwar period were much more important than in the 1900–43 era. Because fewer data are available on these bonds, determination of quality trends is more difficult than for public offerings. Nevertheless, a search of available information indicated, first, that defaults and losses were extremely sparse in the postwar period; but second, that there occurred over the period a noticeable drift of direct placements from extremely high-grade categories to bonds merely considered acceptable as "investment grade." Similarly, there was some increase in the proportion of direct placements considered below investment grade, although the proportion remained much smaller than the corresponding figure for public issues.

4. As judged by agency ratings, public offerings have followed an irregular trend in quality in the postwar period, but are superior to those prior to World War II. Direct offerings are of better quality than public offerings as measured by agency rating divisions into investment and subinvestment grades. For all corporate bonds, agency ratings indicated higher quality and less irregularity in the postwar than in the prewar period; however, by 1965 the proportion rated high grade had drifted down to the 1943 level.

5. Agency ratings of public offerings are not consistently related to postwar business cycles. In two cycles quality has a positive conformity and in two an inverse conformity. Weakening in quality is seemingly not related to the volume of bond offerings.

6. Quality of public offerings as measured by fixed-charge coverage before taxes generally improved over the period 1900–46 and then decreased. Since data for direct offerings are not available for 1944–50, all that can be said is that the peak for all offerings occurred either in the mid-forties or mid-fifties.

7. Direct placements generally had higher earnings coverage than public offerings as a group because of differences in the industry mix.

Industrials, which form the majority of direct placements, usually had higher coverage than utility and transportation issues. In each major industry group, however, directly placed issues had lower coverage than public offerings.

8. Bond quality is sometimes measured by the difference between market yield and a basic interest rate representing the return on essentially risk-free investment. During most of the postwar period, the quality of public offerings was better than in the prewar period in that a larger proportion of issues was offered to yield less than 1 per cent above the "basic yield." While quality as indicated by this measure had slipped by the 1956–59 period to about the level of the late 1920's, the drive for yield in the early 1960's apparently caused most issues to be rated as high grade by this measure. This drive for yield in recent years casts doubt on this means of measuring quality.

9. For virtually the entire postwar period the proportion of bond offerings that were unsecured has been at or near record highs. This is not considered to be a significant factor affecting quality, however.

10. During the postwar period, bonds convertible into stock have frequently constituted 10 to 15 per cent of all bond issues. In neither the prewar nor the postwar period have convertibles had as good earnings-coverage as non-convertibles, and ratings by agencies have indicated a substantial proportion of convertibles are of poor quality. This judgment was generally confirmed by higher default rates among convertibles in the prewar period, although not in the postwar period. As measured by agency rating, convertible bonds have, moreover, apparently fallen in quality from the early to the late postwar period.

Even after this brief listing of the major findings of the study, the question again arises, Has the quality of credit deteriorated? The study aims to answer this question, and examines many different statistical series in the process. There are frequent contradictions in the data and there are obvious cases where certain classes of bonds are substitutes for others, so that partial analysis is likely to be misleading. To remedy this, Charts 1 and 2 present the principal relevant statistical series on the quality of corporate bonds.

Certain obvious conclusions follow from examination of these charts, which show quality improvement over time as a rising trend and, conversely, deterioration as a falling trend. The first is that quality,

CHART 1

Measures of Corporate Bond Quality,
Public and Direct Offerings, 1900–65

Source

1. 1900–43: Hickman, *Volume of Corporate Bond Financing,* Table A-19 divided by Table A-21; 1944–65: Table 21 of this study, new defaults divided by bonds in good standing.
2. 1908–43: Hickman, *Statistical Measures,* Table 52; 1944–65: Tables B-1, B-2, and B-3 of this study.
3. 1900–43: Computed from Hickman, *Statistical Measures,* Table 79; 1951–61: Combination of Table 24 of this study for public offerings and unpublished data of Avery B. Cohan's for direct placements weighted by this study's industrial and public utility (including transportation) direct placements. Hickman's data are after-tax ratios and have been multiplied by a series of factors computed

Source to Chart 1 (continued)

from *Statistics of Income* data on nonfinancial corporations to put them on a before-tax basis. Data for direct placements are unavailable for 1944–50 and after 1951.
4. 1900–43: Hickman, *Statistical Measures*, Table 70; 1944–65: Table E-1 of this study (percentage of rated bonds only).
5. 1900–43: Hickman, *Statistical Measures*, Table 85; 1944–65: Table D-1 of this study.

CHART 2

Low-Grade Bond Offerings as Percentage of Total Rated, 1944–65
(inverted scale)

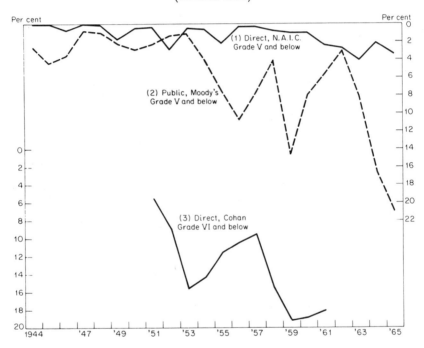

Source: Lines 1 and 2 from Table 15 of this study; line 3 from Cohan, "Yields on Direct Placements, 1951–61," in preparation.

by most of the ex ante measures used, has improved, and now stands appreciably above the levels that prevailed from 1900 through the mid-1930's. Likewise, although most of the measures have shown some deterioration in the postwar period, all except those designated as investment grade were higher in 1965 than in 1943. The available evidence suggests that both direct placement and public offering quality have deteriorated in the last few years analyzed (Chart 1). An exception is times charges earned before taxes. This measure, which combines public offerings and direct placements, has a gap for the years 1944–50 and 1962–65 because earnings ratios are not available in those years for the latter series. The fragmentary data suggest an upward trend, possibly through the mid-forties or fifties, followed by a downward drift.

I

BOND QUALITY: THE SETTING
OF THE PROBLEM

The Prewar Record

In 1958 W. Braddock Hickman's *Corporate Bond Quality and Investor Experience* [1] was published as the second of three volumes in the National Bureau's Studies in Corporate Bond Financing. Hickman examined yields and loss rates on domestic corporate bonds over the years 1900–43, tested different measures of ex ante bond quality against default and loss experience, and estimated yields realized on defaulted bonds for various holding periods. Thus the investor was able to determine what his net gain or loss would have been from investing in bonds of various characteristics and holding them for various periods.

The material for the Hickman study was all "straight corporate bonds" of $5 million or more, issued from 1900 through 1943, plus a 10 per cent sample of issues below that size. Straight bonds are those with fixed income and a single maturity date. Income and serial bonds and all equipment trust certificates were eliminated from the main part of the study because of the complex task of determining the actual yields, as were real estate and finance company bonds.

One of Hickman's most important findings is that, broadly speaking, a diversified portfolio of second-quality issues, even after consideration of default and loss experience, returned a higher yield than a first-quality portfolio. [2]

Hickman noted that several measures of prospective bond quality were relatively efficient indicators of risk of default. Thus, of the bonds issued from 1900 through 1943, the default rate of those rated by agencies in the worst class at offering was seven times that of the best class. [3] Bonds classified in the worst class according to market rating [4]

---

[1] Princeton University Press for National Bureau of Economic Research, 1958.

[2] See the discussion in Chapter VI.

[3] See *Corporate Bond Quality*, Table 1, pp. 10–11. The agency rating is a composite of the ratings assigned by the investment agencies: Moody's, Fitch, and Standard and Poor's. (Before 1941 separate ratings were given by Poor's and by Standard Statistics.)

[4] The market rating is the difference between the yield of a specified bond and the yield of the highest-quality issues of comparable maturity.

had a default rate three times as large as those rated in the best. The default rate of those that earned their fixed charges the least number of times (the lowest times-charges-earned ratio) was seventeen times as large as the rate of those earning their charges the most times. This over-all experience masked considerably better predictive ability for the various quality measures in particular time periods and given industries. Hickman concedes that the measures are not perfect. He says, "The principal errors of judgment committed by the rating systems arose from a failure to appraise accurately the earnings trends of the different industries and to allow fully for cyclical risks." [5] In spite of this difficulty, these measures of prospective bond quality appear relatively efficient.

More important from the standpoint of the present study are Hickman's findings relating to trends and cycles in observed measures of quality. He found in the 1900–43 data both significant long-term trends and shorter-term cyclical movements bearing a definite relationship to conventional business cycles. When "life-span" default rates [6] are classified by year of offering, both movements are visible.

Hickman suggests that bonds issued in times of relatively high business activity tend to have higher default rates than those offered in years of relatively low activity. He also found that bonds issued in the early 1920's and in the period 1935–43 had the lowest life-span default rates. We have been able to confirm his belief that the record of defaults after 1944 would not change this finding, although up to now there has not been a real test. Bonds issued in the first decade of the century and in 1928–29 and 1933 showed the worst life-span default rates. Hickman reasoned that the tendency of default rates to be high for bonds issued in periods of heavy financing connected with major business cycle movements probably resulted from the fact that "in periods of overconfidence, marginal issues were floated that would not have found a ready market when business was depressed." [7] He noted too that the investment agencies also followed a cyclical course in rating bonds, particularly over the short cycles commonly identified with inventory movements. This is of great importance to the present study since, broadly speaking, the postwar period has so far produced

[5] *Ibid.*, p. 13.

[6] The percentage of par amounts of bond offerings going to default at any time in their "life spans."

[7] *Ibid.*, p. 23.

several short or inventory cycles but no recognizable major cycles.

Hickman also notes that, "Viewed in full perspective, the period of the late twenties and early thirties appears as simply a sharp break in a falling trend in default and loss rates." [8] His prospective measures of quality also show a long-term trend toward improvement, especially for public utility issues. The proportion of par amounts offered bearing superior agency ratings generally rose during the forty-four years analyzed. Earnings coverage of bonds also improved. Contrary indications were generally explained by the miserable performance of railroad and industrial corporation issues in the thirties. While caution is warranted in drawing conclusions over a span of years terminated by seemingly unusual depression years when both the small volume of financing and the reactions from previous catastrophic losses had been evident, it will be worth observing whether the data for the period after 1943 also suggest a long-term improvement in bond quality.

The Postwar Study, Sources and Methods

Data for public offerings were obtained from Moody's *Bond Survey,* which lists current offerings. These are essentially complete, although, for the purpose of comparison with data on the prewar years, income bonds, equipment trust certificates, real estate and finance company bonds, and foreign obligations were eliminated by editing for most tabulations. Serial issues were also eliminated in some tabulations in conformity with the Hickman practice. Table 1 shows the comparison between public offerings tabulated here and those listed by the Securities and Exchange Commission, with virtually all of the difference being accounted for by income issues.

The problem of determining the adequacy of coverage for direct placements is more complex than that for public offerings. For the greatest part of the period analyzed in the earlier study, direct placements were almost negligible; only from the middle 1930's on did they become important. Even here the direct placements were relatively uncomplicated, compared to the larger public offerings. In the postwar period, however, not only the increase in volume of direct offerings but the proliferation of types of such instruments greatly increased the problem of analyzing quality. A few illustrations of this point will make

8 *Ibid.,* p. 102.

TABLE 1

Offerings Studied as Proportion of Aggregate Domestic Corporate
Bonds, Excluding Financial and Real Estate Issues, 1948-65
(per cent)

Year of Offerings	Publicly Offered Bonds (1)	Directly Placed Bonds (2)
1948	78.2	68.5
1949	82.0	75.7
1950	86.8	83.1
1951	82.9	84.5
1952	86.5	78.6
1953	90.9	82.8
1954	91.0	86.8
1955	83.7	92.0
1956	86.9	94.8
1957	89.5	99.3
1958	95.2	78.2
1959	92.0	90.9
1960	91.9	93.4
1961	90.0	92.5
1962	90.7	101.6
1963	90.5	100.3
1964	87.3	100.8
1965	91.8	88.8
Total	88.9	89.5

Source: Col. 1: Table A-1, col. 4 ÷ col. 3; col. 2: Table A-1, col. 8 ÷ col. 7.

clear why the problem of quality comparisons of direct placements over time has proved so difficult.

Hickman excluded corporate bonds with serial payment provisions from most of his tabulations on quality because he was interested in yield in relation to quality; yield computation is frequently difficult for bonds which are repaid in instalments. The exclusion of serials made little difference in the pre-World War II years; but following the war, omitting them would have cut the volume by almost half. Blanket exclusion of serials was therefore unjustified in the postwar period, though it meant that strict comparability was not preserved. They are included here. Finally, the postwar period experienced a proliferation of financing methods which has played hob with Hickman's rigid classification of bond characteristics. One can question whether bonds for real estate developments such as shopping centers should be excluded, as they were. The security for these bonds essentially consisted of leases with major national retailing firms which, had they chosen to build directly, would have financed the construction by debentures that would have been included under the Hickman definition. Likewise, should consumer finance company long-term notes be excluded when the borrower was merely a "captive" finance company of a major U.S. durable-goods manufacturer?

Table 1 also compares total direct placements analyzed in this study with the volume recorded by the Securities and Exchange Commission. Differences between totals in this study and the SEC figures are principally caused by lack of publicity about many direct offerings. Our source probably excluded some offerings and included others which were negotiated but not taken down in the year stated or were taken down by banks.[9] In spite of these problems, from 1948 to 1965, 89.5 per cent of the SEC compilation of direct placements is analyzed here. Additional evidence from even more limited studies is also cited at various relevant points.

Evaluation of the Findings

Apart from problems of comparability, how good is the totality of evidence cited here on bond quality in the postwar period? First, let us admit that the quality of a debt instrument cannot be judged independently of the conditions to which it is subject during its life. Thus in Chapter III, where the postwar default record of bonds is discussed, any absolute judgment that the low incidence of default justifies the conclusion of better quality in postwar than prewar bond offerings is obviously questionable. Clearly intertemporal judgments are most difficult in this area. Ex post measures of bond quality—defaults, losses,

---

[9] A search was made in Moody's manuals for all direct offerings of $10 million or more (and some smaller ones) listed in the *Investment Dealers' Digest* to avoid such erroneous inclusions, but information was not always available.

changes in contract terms—for the most part do not tell how bonds differ in quality over time. Somewhat better are ex ante measures such as earnings coverage, security, and perhaps agency ratings. Here again, however, it is hard to make a priori comparisons of quality over time when conditions are not the same. To illustrate, greater stability of income in the postwar period may mean a given earnings coverage affords greater protection to bondholders now than it would have thirty years ago. Likewise, given security provisions may be more useful in reducing default in the postwar period than they were in the prewar period. Finally, judgments taking into account many factors, such as those embodied in the agency rating, may change quality implications over time even though the definition of Aaa bonds, for example, does not change. In terms of defaults or losses, may not bonds rated Baa in the 1960's be equivalent to Aa offerings of the late 1920's, even though characteristics of coverage, security, and so forth are grossly different? Clearly, part of the quality judgment concerns not the inherent characteristic of the bond but the conditions of the economy— will future depressions be less severe?

One aspect of the quality problem has not been faced up to at all— the question of valuation of losses and the possibility of offsets by gains. For example, an institutional investor may suffer losses on some investments, which may be offset by unexpected gains on other assets. Hickman found the presence of a substantial number of bonds redeemed prior to maturity at a call premium. The result was a substantial windfall gain which, according to Hickman's calculations, increased the realized yield of lower-rated issues above that of prime-quality issues.[10]

It is possible that the total returns realized on issues bearing convertible rights, warrants, and other noninterest benefits in the postwar period should be taken into account in determining the quality of bond offerings. Quite likely many investors have realized benefits from convertibles and warrants attached to bonds out of all proportion to their losses on bond offerings.

Finally, in this compilation of factors making for problems in judging quality, one step has been taken as given—the relation between ex ante

---

[10] This finding has been challenged by Harold Fraine, who suggests that the premium on bonds called prior to maturity should be offset against the lower yields available on reinvestment at reduced rates. See Harold G. Fraine and Robert H. Mills, "Effect of Defaults and Credit Deterioration on Yields of Corporate Bonds," *The Journal of Finance*, September 1961, pp. 423–434.

and ex post quality measures. For this, reliance has been placed on the evidence produced by Hickman, although it is not known whether this judgment is valid. It may be that intangibles of credit selection, amortization of principal payments, and contract modification have substantially changed the default and loss likelihood of bonds of given characteristics when judged by earnings coverage, agency rating, security, and market rating. Here it is particularly important to note that the three factors listed above—credit selection, amortization of principal, and contract modification—are closely associated with the greatly enlarged practice since prewar times of placing bond issues directly with the ultimate holders.

Practically all direct placements have some prepayment provision, whether in the form of serial maturities or sinking funds. Because of the small number of holders, the distinction is almost meaningless and often cannot be made from the available information. To maintain comparability with the Hickman study, which includes straight bonds placed publicly or privately (directly), with or without sinking fund provisions, but excludes serial bonds, separate tabulations have been provided which include and exclude direct placements. The exclusion of direct placements reduces the total par amount by over 40 per cent. Publicly placed serial bonds were issued in very small amounts after 1943 and have been included in certain tables. While the prepayment arrangements may have had an effect on the relation between ex ante and ex post measures of quality, this effect may not have been much different from that of the many sinking fund bonds issued in the twenties, thirties, and early forties.

A final word is necessary about terminology and measurement. Most of the tables have gone back to 1944 and 1945 in order to link up with Hickman's data, and use of the term "postwar" should be understood to include these war years. It has been necessary to make a few comparisons using a smaller number of years, since the data, for the most part compiled by government agencies, did not cover the full period.

In the light of incomplete data, a changed composition of bonds, and economic conditions quite different from the prewar period, how can the reliability of this study be evaluated? We are fairly well convinced that our conclusions on quality changes in the postwar period are correct. We are less sure of the comparisons with earlier periods, but by no measure reject the evidence that quality in general has improved. Finally, we are quite unsure of the absolute measures of quality; i.e., that 95.6 per cent of all bonds offered in the postwar period are of investment quality or that only 0.2 per cent of postwar bond issues have defaulted. These are our own evaluations; the reader is cautioned not to treat the findings uncritically.

Characteristics of Postwar Bond Financing

The early postwar years were characterized by growing public confidence—though not completely without doubts—that financial affairs and institutions' practices were fundamentally "sound." While a recognizable undercurrent of speculation flourished at times, considerable progress seemed to have been made both in perfecting the tools of investment analysis and the institutions themselves, as compared with the 1920's. Until the late 1950's, it is probably fair to say, few doubts assailed investors. Sharp breaks in the stock market in connection with President Eisenhower's health; the development of Russian space vehicles; failure or near failure of major commercial real estate developments; the collapse of the new-issue market in 1962; isolated brokerage, savings-and-loan, and banking failures; and greater foreclosures in mortgage markets all add to the feeling that perhaps conditions are basically less changed than generally realized. Still, the corporate bond area has been relatively untouched by the failures that earlier plagued this financing instrument.

Table 2 shows that in the years 1948–65 corporate bond offerings totaled $122.4 billion, or over 70 per cent more than was offered in the period 1900–43. This is all the more remarkable because of the ability of firms to generate their own capital, as will be seen later. A major change had also occurred by industry. Railroad offerings and even those of other transportation firms in the postwar period had become only a minor part of the total instead of one-quarter as in the earlier period.[11] Utility offerings constituted almost the same proportion in these two periods. Since, as Hickman has shown, railroad bonds were quite distinctive both in ex ante measures and in ultimate quality experience, the virtual disappearance of straight bond obligations of railroads helps

[11] Equipment trust certificates are omitted throughout this paper as they were in the prewar study. They are generally of much shorter maturity and the specific security more easily liquidated than true railroad bonds. For this reason, their exclusion is felt to be legitimate.

TABLE 2

Major Differences in Prewar and Postwar Corporate
Bond Offerings, 1900-65
(dollars in millions)

	1900-43	Per Cent	1948-65	Per Cent
Industry composition				
Railroads (transportation)	18,595	26.0	13,933	11.4
Public utilities	33,426	46.7	53,749	43.9
Industrials	19,523	27.3	54,682	44.7
All offerings	71,544	100.0	122,364	100.0
Public and direct placements				
Public offerings	66,425	92.8	66,045	54.0
Direct placements	5,119	7.2	56,319	46.0
All offerings	71,544	100.0	122,364	100.0
Convertibles and nonconvertibles[a]			1956-65	
Convertibles	7,088	9.9	7,418	7.7
Nonconvertibles	64,456	90.1	89,311	92.3
All offerings	71,544	100.0	96,729	100.0

Source: W. Braddock Hickman, *The Volume of Corporate Bond Financing since 1900*, Princeton for NBER, 1953, Table A-10, pp. 284 ff., and *Statistical Measures of Corporate Bond Financing since 1900*, Princeton for NBER, 1960, Table 118, p. 211; and SEC, June 1966 release on Corporate Securities Offered for Cash in the United States and various releases in Statistical Series on Corporate Securities Offered for Cash Sale.

[a]Convertible = convertible into common stock. The data on convertibles and nonconvertibles include bonds of financial and real estate issuers, which are excluded from other sections of the table.

to explain some of the observed changes in bond quality between the two periods.

The most important difference between bond offerings in the 1900–43 period and later was the development of direct offerings. Whereas only 7 per cent of all bond offerings in the earlier period had been placed directly, a shade under half of the value of corporate bond issues in the postwar period were directly placed. As Table 3 shows, direct place-

TABLE 3

Direct Placements as Percentage of Total Bond Offerings, 1900-65

Period	Per Cent
1900-09	2.8
1910-19	3.8
1920-29	0.6
1930-33	2.2
1934-39	16.6
1940-49	32.7
1950-59	42.8
1960-65	50.4

Source: 1900-39: Hickman, *Volume of Corporate Bond Financing*, Table A-10, pp 284 f. (straight bonds only); 1940-49: *ibid.*, plus this study's Table G-1; 1950-65: Table A-1 (SEC figures for Total Minus Financial and Real Estate).

ments were insignificant before the enactment of the Securities Act of 1933, when they immediately became important and have continued gradually to increase.

Other comparisons between prewar and postwar bond offerings are more difficult to come by. It is interesting to note, however, that the general impression that convertible bonds have been much more important than formerly is not sustained by the evidence, admittedly covering less than the full span of postwar years. There is little difference in the proportion of bond issues that are convertible into common stocks for the two periods, as may be seen in Table 2.

Not only the types of corporate bonds have changed since the period covered by Hickman; bonds have also changed in their relative importance in the economy. Large as the absolute value of bond financing was in the postwar period, it was becoming a relatively less important means of financing. Table 4 shows for the period 1946–65 that bonds and notes constituted 10 per cent of nonfinancial corporation financing in comparison with 20.5 per cent in the 1901–12 period, 14 per cent from 1923 to 1929, and an actual negative figure (because of net retirements) in the 1930's. The major offsetting change that has occurred to make up for the diminished sale of corporate bonds has been greater internal financing (except in the 1934–39 period) and greater use of

TABLE 4

Structural Changes in Sources of Financing of
Nonfinancial Corporations, 1901-65

Source of Financing	Percentage of Total Source of Funds			
	1901-12 (1)	1923-29 (2)	1934-39 (3)	1946-65 (4)
Internal				
Total	55.2	54.7	97.6	69.6
Capital consumption allow.	37.9	39.8	124.8	43.7
Net saving	17.3	14.9	-27.3	25.9
External				
Total	44.8	45.3	2.4	30.4
Borrowing, total	30.8	25.9	-6.6	26.7
Short-term	8.0	4.3	1.0	14.2
Long-term	22.5	21.6	-7.6	12.5
Bonds and notes	20.5	14.2	-5.2	9.6
Mortgages	2.0	7.4	-2.4	3.0
Equity securities	14.0	19.4	9.0	3.7
Total	100.0	100.0	100.0	100.0
Total (billion dollars)	40.0	86.1	28.9	831.8

Source: Cols. 1–3: all except long-term borrowing from Raymond
W. Goldsmith, *The Flow of Capital Funds in the Postwar Economy,*
New York, NBER, 1965, Table 37; bonds and notes and mortgages,
computed from Goldsmith, *Financial Intermediaries in the American
Economy Since 1900,* Princeton for NBER, 1958, Table 53. Col. 4:
Board of Governors of the Federal Reserve System, Flow of Funds,
Table 4D, in May 1966 *Bulletin;* F/F Levels, May 3, 1966; F/F An-
nual, November 6, 1965, and 1963 Supplement. Short-term borrowing
includes bank loans, n.e.c., trade debt, and an estimated portion of
other loans. The remainder is included in bonds and notes.
Note: Figures do not necessarily add to total because of rounding.

short debt (bank and trade loans). Of all external financing, however,
bonds now constitute about one-third, surprisingly close to their importance in the 1920's although less so than in the 1901–12 period.

One more comparison will show how significant these findings are.
Table 5 shows what proportion long-term corporate debt represents

TABLE 5

*Relative Importance of Selected Components of Public and
Private Debt, Selected Years, 1916-65*
(per cent)

Year	Corporate Long-Term Debt	Individual and Noncorporate Mortgage Debt (Nonfarm)	Federal Debt	State and Local Debt
1916	3.5	10.2	1.5	5.4
1921	24.9	9.4	17.0	4.8
1926	24.7	14.2	11.4	6.3
1931	27.7	17.0	10.2	8.5
1936	23.6	13.5	20.9	9.0
1941	20.6	12.9	26.6	7.7
1946	10.4	8.2	5.8	3.4
1951	12.7	12.9	4.2	4.4
1956	14.1	17.1	31.9	6.0
1961	15.8	20.1	26.2	6.9
1965	16.4	22.5	21.3	7.3

Source: U.S. Department of Commerce, Bureau of the Census
Historical Statistics of the U.S., Colonial Times to 1957, Washington,
1960, p. 664; and *Survey of Current Business,* May 1966, p. 12.

of public and private debt at the beginning of each five-year period
since the series originated in 1916. If these figures are correct, corporate
long-term debt is nowhere near as large a factor in the total debt structure as it was when America entered World War II, although it has
been creeping up slightly in the postwar period. On the other hand,
mortgage debt of individuals is considerably higher than in 1941.

It has been difficult to provide a direct comparison with Hickman's
study to determine how bond quality compares prewar and postwar,
and at the same time to describe accurately the quality characteristics
of contemporary corporate bonds. The question arises, if Hickman's
simplifying steps, such as the elimination of serial bonds, lack of specific
examination of convertibles and warrants, and exclusion of finance and
real estate bonds, are also followed in the postwar period, how representative is the area studied of the universe of corporate bonds?

This is known: corporate bonds are a less important means of financing business than they were in the period prior to the 1930's, when internal funds were less adequate. Corporate bonds are also a smaller proportion of public and private debt.

In view of the problems of this study, what can be said about the accuracy of the general findings? Probably the changes indicated here are in the correct direction, but judgments as to absolute quality levels of bond instruments or of institutional holdings of such bonds *en masse* are hazardous. At best, the hazard of financial catastrophe arising from unsoundness of corporate bonds is probably less than it has been in previous times, not only because most quality indicators, as will be seen, give indication that bonds are better instruments than during some years of the prewar period but also because neither the relative importance of corporate bonds as a financing medium nor their importance as a part of the investment structure is as great as in the Hickman period.

The major development in the corporate bond field in the postwar period has been the growth of direct placements. These offerings, being essentially private contracts between the borrower and lender, have less homogeneity than, and in many other respects do not resemble, public offerings. In any case, there are few data in public sources describing them. For this reason, a major effort has been made to compile and describe a number of quality measures of direct placements and to do what could be done to make these measures comparable to those available on public issues. If this task were not undertaken, it could be legitimately charged that our statements on quality referred to only part of the universe of corporate bonds.

II

DIRECT PLACEMENTS
VERSUS PUBLIC OFFERINGS

Because of the greatly increased importance of direct placements now as compared with the Hickman era, the task of analyzing the quality of these issues is crucial to the entire study. This chapter explains those characteristics of directly placed issues that are important to quality, and the prewar history of these bonds; it then examines what evidence is available on their postwar quality.

Volume and Characteristics

As was indicated earlier, the most profound change in the corporate bond market in the postwar period has been the coming of age of direct placements as distinguished from underwritten issues offered to the public at large.[1] Direct placements have considerable advantages to the borrower and even more to the lender. The borrower, in effect, trades a slightly higher rate of interest for flexibility and assured financing.[2] The lender receives possibly a higher rate of interest in return for relinquishing some degree of marketability.

The result of these advantages has been a great increase in the proportion of bond issues classified as direct placements. From 1900 to 1943, the period covered by Hickman's study, direct placements of cash offerings constituted only 7.2 per cent of the total amount reaching the market.[3] From 1948–65 the corresponding proportion was 46.0 per cent (see Table 2).

The development of direct placements has important implications for a study of corporate bond quality. It is really not the degree of "publicness" of a bond that has much to do with ultimate quality but

[1] The National Bureau of Economic Research now uses the term "direct placement" to indicate bonds not marketed to the general public. The Hickman study defined private placements as those with less than twenty-five investors participating. Neither term is strictly correct, since bonds not offered generally to the market are not necessarily private nor directly made.

[2] See George T. Conklin, Jr., "Direct Placements," *Journal of Finance*, June 1951, pp. 85–118.

[3] Hickman, *Volume of Corporate Bond Financing*, p. 94, Table 8.

rather other attributes that tend to be associated with the method of marketing the obligation. Since nearly all direct placements are taken by large institutions fully able to judge bond quality, publicity that might otherwise be a safeguard presumably is not missed. Furthermore, many institutions purchasing direct placements can forgo the added liquidity of public issues because of the forecastable nature of their cash needs. Indeed, insurance companies are by far the largest purchasers of direct placements. The development of direct placements, however, has led to a large informational gap. In the first place, some direct placements fail to receive any public notice, and those that are announced may have undisclosed terms. Second, only a small percentage of corporate direct placements receive ratings from the recognized agencies, although those sold to insurance companies do receive presumably comparable ratings. Third, market rating measures may not reflect the collective judgment of the market place about the proper yield of the security, but instead may be a matter of negotiation heavily influenced by bargaining position and ability. Finally, because of the ease in changing contracts, what otherwise might be a default may in a direct placement simply become an unpublicized contract modification. Therefore, it should be understood that measurement of quality for direct placements is considerably more difficult than for public offerings.

The Prewar Experience

The quality of direct placements in the 1920's and 1930's is encouraging. Table 6 shows that, on the average, 0.15 per cent of the

TABLE 6

Direct Placements and All Corporate Bonds, Percentage of Outstandings Defaulting, 1920-39
(average annual rates)

Period of Default	Direct Placements	All Bonds
1920-29	0.15	0.95
1930-39	1.22	3.20

Source: Hickman, *Volume of Corporate Bond Financing*, Table 22, p. 208, and data compiled by Corporate Bond Research Project, on file at NBER.

outstanding private placements defaulted each year during the 1920's and 1.22 per cent each year during the 1930's, substantially below the comparable figures for all corporate bonds.

As might be expected, there are some distortions in the above comparisons, not the least of which was that because of the small volume of private placements defaulting, only three years during the 1920's (1923, 1924, and 1929) witnessed any private placement defaults, and in these particular three years the proportion of outstandings defaulting was close to 1 per cent. In the 1930's defaults as a percentage of outstandings were much higher. Defaults approached 4 per cent of outstandings for direct placements in 1935, even though the average for the decade was only slightly over 1 per cent.

Similar deceptive default rates occur when the comparison is on direct placements defaulting by year of offering. In individual years of the 1920's these were quite high (actually 100 per cent in 1929) simply because of the paucity of direct placement offerings in any one year. There were, however, only three years of the 1920's containing direct placement offerings that defaulted. With only a trickle of directly placed offerings in the 1920's, some 28.9 per cent of the offerings volume went to default. The reconciliation of low default rates calculated on outstandings and high default rates calculated on offerings for direct placements in the 1920's can be made when it is realized that offerings of direct placements were in much heavier volume in the period prior to the 1920's than in the 1920's themselves (see Hickman, *Volume of Corporate Bond Financing*, Table A-10, pp. 284–285).

TABLE 7

Percentage of Corporate Bond Offerings Bearing Agency Ratings of I-IV, Direct Placements and All Bonds, 1910-39

Period of Offerings	Direct Placements	All Bonds
1910-19	85.8	80.5
1920-29	97.9	80.7
1930-39	84.0	80.2

Source: Computed from Hickman, *Corporate Bond Quality*, Table 34, p. 179, and data compiled by Corporate Bond Research Project on file at NBER.

TABLE 8

Default Rates on Offerings of Direct Placements and
All Bonds, by Agency Rating Grades, 1910-39
(percentage of par amount going to default)

| Period of Offerings | Grades I-IV | | Grades V-IX | |
	Direct Placements	All Bonds	Direct Placements	All Bonds
1910-19	25.4	25.8	98.2	46.0
1920-29	28.8	15.2	0[a]	44.6
1930-39	1.0	7.0	56.0	37.1

Source: Computed from Hickman, *Corporate Bond Quality,* Table 34, p. 179, and data compiled by Corporate Bond Research Project on file at NBER.

[a]Based on only three issues.

Direct placements in the prewar period commanded a slightly higher agency rating than all corporate bonds, as may be seen from Table 7. The period of greatest difference in quality was obviously that of 1920–29, when nearly all direct placements were rated as investment grade in comparison with about four-fifths of all corporate bonds.

The agencies apparently have had a fair record in determining the quality of direct placement bonds, as may be seen by the much higher default rates for low-rated bonds than for bonds bearing a high agency rating (Table 8). On the other hand, it is curious that in the 1920–29 period highly rated direct placements had worse default rates than all corporate bonds. Undoubtedly of greatest relevance to postwar experience is the showing of the 1930–39 period, when direct placements receiving investment quality ratings in grades I–IV showed substantially lower losses than did all bonds offered in the period.[4]

During the first two decades of the century, direct placements tended to be loans to firms with slightly lower earnings coverage than those whose bonds were publicly offered, but this was not the case for the period 1920–39. It is clear from Table 9 that by the decade of the

---

[4] In 1930–36 direct placements comprised less than 10 per cent of the total volume of offerings, but by 1939 they approached 30 per cent of total offerings (see Hickman, *Volume of Corporate Bond Financing,* Table A-10).

TABLE 9

*Average Times-Charges-Earned Coverage of Direct Placements
and Public Offerings, 1900-39*

Period of Offerings	Direct Placements	Public Offerings
1900-09	1.31	1.55
1910-19	1.75	1.93
1920-29	2.34	2.01
1930-39	4.05	2.55

Source: Data compiled by Corporate Bond Research Project, on file at NBER.

1930's the direct placement earnings coverage was considerably better than that for public offerings.

Direct placements of given quality, it has been noted, are likely to bear higher yields than public offerings simply because lack of marketability, lower issuing costs, and reduction of marketing uncertainty warrant such treatment. This tendency inevitably should affect the tabulations of direct placements according to market rating. Actually, a greater proportion of direct placements than public offerings bore yields at offering within one percentage point (100 basis points) of the basic corporate bond yield in the last three decades of the prewar era, suggesting that most direct placements were of relatively high quality (see Table 10).

TABLE 10

*Percentage of Direct Placements and Public Offerings with
High Grade Market Ratings, 1900-39*

Period of Offerings	Direct Placements	Public Offerings
1900-09	24.77	43.40
1910-19	50.42	34.61
1920-29	81.80	35.99
1930-39	74.04	60.94

Source: Same as Table 9.

Except for the decade of the 1920's, direct placements have relied less upon specific security than have publicly offered obligations (Table 11). It is one advantage of the direct placement method that, with perhaps more access to information about the company, the investor may require less of the conventional assurances of repayment such as specific security. Moreover, direct placements may add negative pledges, working capital covenants, and other detailed provisions not present in public issues.

TABLE 11

Proportion Secured Bonds Are of All Direct Placements and Public Offerings, 1900-39

	Per Cent Secured	
Period of Offerings	Direct Placements	Public Offerings
1900-09	51.69	87.39
1910-19	69.67	80.67
1920-29	72.06	68.32
1930-39	66.14	68.40

Source: Same as Table 9.

As a group, direct placements achieved a favorable default record as compared with the universe of all bonds, and almost all ex ante measures of quality favored them. This is not to say, however, that direct placements are not vulnerable to economic adversity, as they indeed showed in the middle 1930's.

Direct Placements in the Postwar Period

Direct placements came into their own in the postwar period. They increased in importance during the 1930's principally because corporations, fearing failure of their bond offerings in the uncertain markets of those years, turned to direct negotiations with one or a small group of purchasers. In the postwar period, however, the direct placement route became a growing means of financing not dictated from necessity. Table 2 shows that from 1948 to 1965 direct placements were 46.0 per cent of all offerings in comparison with only about 7 per cent in the years from 1900 to 1943. According to the data compiled by the Securities and Exchange Commission (and shown in Table A-1 of this study), these nonmarketed issues accounted for over half of the total nonfinancial corporate bond and note issues in five of the eighteen years ended in 1965.

A definitional problem inhibits precise comparability of the postwar data with prewar data on direct placement quality. Hickman's study of bond quality was largely confined to so-called straight bonds, i.e., issues with the interest payment not contingent upon income and, most important, containing a single maturity date. The exclusion of serial bonds from Hickman's study was necessary in order to allow calculation of yields which otherwise became vastly complex for any substantial number of bonds where most of the information on payment schedules was difficult to obtain. Exclusion of serial bonds had little meaning, however, in the 1900–43 period because of their small volume. In 1925, when serial bond offerings reached their peak in dollar volume for the decade, they accounted for only about 11 per cent of all bond offerings.[5] Not until 1940 was the 1925 volume of serial bonds exceeded, but in that year serials were still only 11 per cent of total bond volume.

The problem begins in the postwar period, when direct placements expanded greatly in volume. Since direct placement is ideally suited to serial payments, or even to payment on an amortized basis, it was no wonder that bonds with multiple dates of principal payments became a sizable proportion of total direct placements. Because serial bonds in the private placement sector have become so important a part of the corporate bond universe, it seems inappropriate to continue to maintain the definitional limitations of "straight" bonds only in analyzing characteristics of quality. In addition, of course, some repayment feature, either sinking fund or serial payment, is a characteristic of direct placements.

Direct Evidence on Postwar Quality

The evidence of quality of direct placements leaves something to be desired. Essentially the reader must decide between series admittedly covering too short a span and those in which the evaluation limit may be an extreme one. In essence, however, the findings of both coincide on the recent direction of quality changes.

[5] *Ibid.,* Tables A-4 and A-1.

The Cohan Data

Avery B. Cohan of the University of North Carolina, who is partici-pating in the National Bureau's study of interest rates, drew a sample of direct placements made by twenty-three life insurance companies and one pension fund during the period 1951–61.[6] The total assets of these companies as of the end of 1959 were 73 per cent of those of the industry, and the companies themselves included most of those active in direct placement lending. Cohan estimates that his sample covered 44 per cent by volume of all direct placements negotiated during the period. He recorded some eighteen characteristics of direct placement offerings, including, of course, amount, maturity, security, industry, size of capitalization, debt ratio, and call protection. One important characteristic was the number of times the fixed charges (including the interest cost on the new debt) are covered by earnings before interest and taxes.

The Cohan sample did not include bonds with warrants or conver-sion features, but it is representative of ordinary direct placements.

Cohan found two variables of notable significance in accounting for yield differences between direct placement issues, earnings coverage, and size of company, and he has classified his offerings by a combina-tion of these two characteristics to obtain quality classes.[7] Thus, his Class 1, or best quality, consisted of issues of firms with capitalization of over $135 million and earnings coverage of over fifteen times for indus-trials and six times and over for utilities. His second class included issues of firms having either (1) capitalization of over $135 million and coverage for industrials of 5.1–15.0 times earnings and for utilities of 4.0–5.9 or (2) capitalization of $45.1–$135.0 million and coverage of over fifteen for industrials and of six and over for utilities. Similar criteria representing combinations of size and earnings coverage were established for five other industrial classes and six other utility classes. This classification system was valid since some correspondence in the behavior of yield existed between Cohan's classes and several of Moody's classes by rating grades. Furthermore, Cohan tested his qual-ity ratings by distributing a sample of 198 agency-rated industrials and

---

[6] I am indebted to Cohan for access to his preliminary tabulations and analyses.

[7] It is by no means clear that the lower yield associated with direct placements to larger firms is a reflection of quality rather than of market power on the part of the borrower. Some, of course, would hold that market power itself and/or the diversity that goes with size are in themselves reflections of quality.

TABLE 12

*Distribution of Number of Public Offerings, by Agency Rating,
Cohan Quality Class, and Industrial Group, 1951-61*
(percentage of each quality class)

Agency Rating	Quality Class					
	1	2	3	4	5[a]	6-8
Aaa						
Industrials	21.2					
Utilities	44.6	3.2				
Aa						
Industrials	56.1	7.9	1.7			
Utilities	45.8	47.6	17.4	16.7	16.7	
A						
Industrials	19.7	78.9	41.4	19.2	—	
Utilities	9.6	47.6	71.7	66.7	50.0	33.3
Baa						
Industrials	3.0	13.2	53.4	61.5	30.0	
Utilities	—	1.6	10.8	16.7	33.3	—
Ba						
Industrials			3.4	19.2	70.0	
Utilities						66.7
Total						
Industrials	100.0	100.0	99.9	99.9	100.0	—
Utilities	100.0	100.0	99.9	100.1	100.0	100.0

Source: Avery B. Cohan, "Yields on Direct Placements, 1951-61,"
National Bureau of Economic Research, in preparation.

[a]5-7 for industrials.

219 utility offerings made publicly in the 1951–61 period. The result, shown in Table 12, indicates the degree of correspondence between agency ratings and Cohan's own quality classifications. The distribution is by number of issues.

Table 13 shows the dollar-value distribution of Cohan's direct placement sample by major grouping of quality grade for 1951–61. There is an irregular swing from the prime grades to the lower grades over the course of the period, but this is in part deceptive because of changes in the middle group as well. A more precise measure of the quality shifts (assuming equal value quality grades) is indicated by Chart 3, which shows the average quality grade for all direct placements in Cohan's sample. Here the quality deterioration is not so pronounced. Indeed, apart from the fact that the two beginning years were relatively high in quality and the last two were years of low quality, it could be said that there was no change in quality based on this measure.

Over the period covered by the data, Cohan's two quality criteria were moving in opposite directions; capitalization was increasing and

TABLE 13

Percentage Distribution of Dollar Value of Direct Placements by Quality Classes, Defined in Terms of Capitalization of Borrowing Firms and Earnings Coverage, 1951-61
(per cent and dollar total)

Year	Quality Classes				Dollar Volume (millions)
	1-3	4-5	6-9	Total	
1951	64.8	29.6	5.6	100.0	2,803
1952	53.4	37.8	8.8	100.0	1,185
1953	29.5	54.9	15.6	100.0	906
1954	44.4	41.3	14.4	100.1	1,417
1955	24.5	63.9	11.5	99.9	1,471
1956	37.5	52.1	10.4	100.0	1,731
1957	31.4	59.1	9.5	100.0	1,187
1958	52.5	32.1	15.5	100.1	1,171
1959	51.7	29.2	19.2	100.1	851
1960	38.4	42.8	18.8	100.0	1,119
1961	25.8	56.3	18.0	100.1	1,097

Source: Cohan, "Yields on Direct Placements."

CHART 3

Average Rating Class for Cohan Sample of Direct Placements, 1951–61

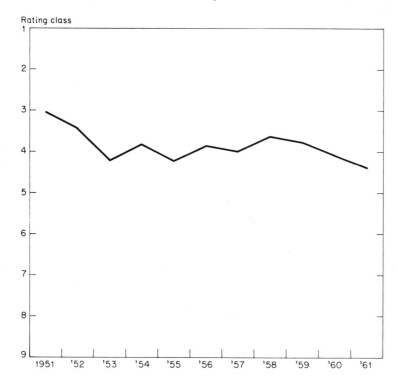

Source: Computed from Cohan, "Yields on Direct Placements."
Note: Rating class is defined by amount of *pro forma* capitalization and *pro forma* interest.

earnings coverage decreasing. The geometric means for the periods 1951–55 and 1956–61 were as follows: [8]

	1951–55	1956–61
Total *pro forma* capitalization (millions of dollars)		
Industrials	12.8	24.9
Public utilities	11.4	16.1
Times charges earned		
Industrials	11.8	8.3
Public utilities	3.1	2.9

Thus, one might expect Cohan's combination quality measure to be somewhat sluggish in indicating long-run trends.

[8] From Cohan, "Yields on Direct Placements, 1951–61."

CHART 4

Earnings Coverage of Direct Offerings Before Taxes, by Industrial Group, 1951–61

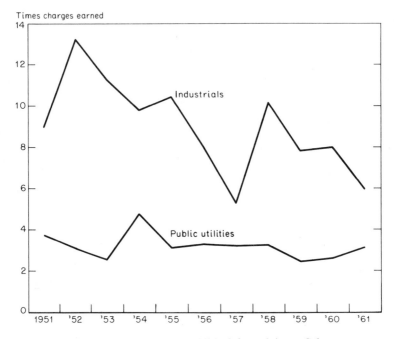

Source: Medians computed from unpublished data of Avery Cohan.

CHART 5

Ratio of Pro Forma *Long-Term Debt to* Pro Forma *Capitalization for Direct Placements, 1951–61*

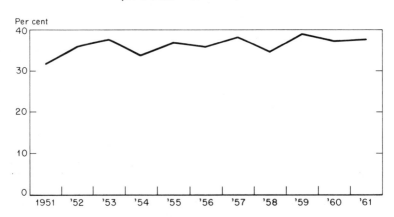

Source: Computed from Cohan, "Yields on Direct Placements."
Note: Average of quarterly means is weighted by dollar volume.

If the quality measure combining size of capitalization and earnings coverage moves in a sluggish manner because of the opposite movements of the characteristics used for classification, what about earnings coverage alone, a more conventional measure than the combination favored by Cohan? Chart 4 indicates his findings for the period and sample he surveyed. The data plotted are medians of annual earnings coverage for direct offerings and are shown separately for industrials and public utilities. While there is some variation in the ratios, in general the chart gives a moderately consistent picture of gradual decline in earnings coverage from 1951 to 1961 for both industry groups. The industrial median in 1951 was about nine times coverage in comparison with about six times coverage in 1961; comparable public utility medians were four times and three times, respectively. The ratios are compared with those for public offerings in Chart 10.

One finding of Cohan's has a direct implication for quality: long-term debt as a proportion of *pro forma* capital showed very little trend. Chart 5 shows the yearly average of the ratio of long-term debt to *pro forma* capitalization. Thus, at least as far as this measure is concerned, there is no real tendency of a change in credit quality.

One more piece of evidence on the quality problem is provided by Cohan. Table 14 compares public offerings and direct placements by

TABLE 14

*Comparison of Public Offerings and Direct Placements
by Cohan Quality Classes, 1951-61*
(percentage distribution by number of offerings)

	Quality Classes						
	1	2	3	4	5[a]	6-8	Total
Industrials							
Public offerings	33.3	19.2	29.3	13.1	5.1	–	100.0
Direct placements	4.3	7.6	16.1	21.5	22.8	27.7	100.0
Public utilities							
Public offerings	37.9	28.8	21.0	8.2	2.7	1.4	100.0
Direct placements	0.8	3.0	8.5	18.7	22.2	46.8	100.0

Source: Cohan, "Yields on Direct Placements."

[a]5-7 for industrials, public offerings.

his quality classes. Obviously, by this distribution, public offerings appear to be of much higher quality than direct placements. But since size was one criterion of Cohan's quality classification, it is possible that the direct placements, which were of smaller size, may have been rated down when in other quality criteria such as coverage they were just as good.

Data of the National Association of Insurance Commissioners

Evidence on the proportion of direct placements that have been considered "investment grade," covering a considerable span of time, is provided by the Committee on Valuation of the National Association of Insurance Commissioners (N.A.I.C.).[9]

In 1910 the National Convention of Insurance Commissioners (predecessor of the N.A.I.C.), through its Committee on Valuation of Securities, began publication of uniform price lists for the purpose of valuing securities in insurance company portfolios. The basis for evaluation at the time was the market price. At roughly the same time, the insurance industry, led by New York companies, was evolving a doctrine that fixed-term, "amply secured" bonds not in default would be valued at cost modified by accrued amortization of discount or premiums. In the 1920's such a method of valuation of fixed-income securities had been adopted by nearly all states.

Because the privilege of adopting a cost basis for valuation (amortized for premium or discount) was only open for "amply secured" bonds in good standing, use of a market-price concept for "nonamortizable" securities caused recurrent valuation problems in each crisis period—1907, 1914, and 1931. With the onset of the Great Depression, the New York State Insurance Department decided that more attention should be paid to the quality of bonds and in 1932 notified companies doing business in that state that only bonds rated in the first five rating grades by one of the rating agencies would be considered eligible for amortization on a cost basis. This measure was not fully satisfactory; during the 1930's the insurance industry was criticized for giving some bonds amortized valuation even though they sold at quite low market prices. In 1940 the N.A.I.C. adopted the following criteria for eligi-

[9] This account is taken from Harold G. Fraine, *Valuation of Securities Holdings of Life Insurance Companies*, Homewood, Ill., 1962, pp. 1–16. Only that part of the valuation process directly applying to quality is here described.

bility: (1) bonds rated in the first four grades by two agencies, (2) bonds rated in the first five grades by three agencies, (3) bonds rated in the first five grades by two agencies and priced at 55 or better in September, October, and November. The last test, that of price, was later changed to a yield spread over U.S. government bonds of 3.9 per cent. Later this was reduced to 1.5 per cent.

In 1948, an industry committee initiated an inquiry into the performance of bond investments as revealed by the National Bureau's Corporate Bond Project, the culminating reports on which were the Hickman study. Evolving out of this study was a two-class reserve scheme for bonds in good standing to cushion differences between cost and market price. Falling in the first class, subject to annual reserve accruals of 0.05 per cent, were corporate bonds in the first four rating grades or equivalent, while all other good bonds were in the second class subject to a 1 per cent accumulation rate. In 1953, the N.A.I.C. specified two tests of eligibility for each class of corporate bonds, as follows:

Test 1: all bonds in the first four rating grades of one of the accredited agencies, or debt ratio of 50 to 75 per cent of total capitalization depending on industry, plus average earnings coverage of 1.5 times before taxes over preceding five years and actual coverage of 1.5 times in either of the last two years.

Test 2: earnings requirements of one times average fixed charges for the last five years and on an actual basis for one of the last two years, and, for railroad bonds, current assets equal to 125 per cent of current liabilities.

Public utility and industrial bonds were to have adjusted earnings equal to mandatory principal payments and sinking-fund requirements (excluding final maturities) in each year, or working capital equal to 100 per cent of long-term debt. Appropriate modifications in each test have been made for new enterprises and for special obligations and guaranteed and contractually supported obligations.[10]

Bonds are currently divided by these ratings into two classes. The first is defined as those bearing either agency ratings in the first four grades, or earnings coverage of 1.5 times five-year average fixed charges

[10] See precise statement of tests in Committee on Valuation of Securities, *Valuation Manual,* New York, 1959. Further slight modifications have been made from time to time which, however, have not altered the basic over-all quality standards demanded of the tests.

plus certain balance sheet conditions dependent in part upon the industry. In the early postwar period, standards for the top class had been defined as those falling in the first four rating grades by two agencies, in the first five by three agencies, or in the first four by two agencies plus a yield spread varying from less than 3.9 per cent over the yield of long-term Treasury bonds, as of the last war years, down to a 1.5 per cent spread in 1950. In 1953, the present standards were adopted. Since only a few of the postwar years were subject to this different standard, our remarks will be confined to the definition of bonds currently passing the first test.

Interviews with bond analysts suggest that few, if any, bonds with five-year earnings coverage of only 1.5 times would, if rated currently, bear agency ratings in the first four grades. While proof is lacking, the impression is received that 1.5 times earnings coverage might be the lower limit of class IV, or Baa, since bonds having other features of strength might conceivably fall into this class. Interviews with the N.A.I.C. staff indicate that the troublesome cases—those bonds clearly deserving Test 1 classification for their equivalence to bonds rated in the first four agency rating grades, but which are unable to show adequate earnings coverage—include many obligations of airline and finance companies. Significantly, both of these industries, because of vigorous growth patterns, have been increasingly heavy borrowers in the late postwar period. N.A.I.C. found a number of bonds, which barely passed the earnings test for Test 1, failed on other grounds—most importantly, the balance sheet conditions.

These ratings provide an objective measure of quality for bonds considered as "investment grade," even though the standards as formally defined do not match those normally used to determine the first four agency ratings. The N.A.I.C. occupies a respected position as an arm of the state supervisory agencies of major financial institutions and as a body of independent analysts taking an objective view of bond quality. The long-term record of bonds rated in its preferred class is a useful time series for analysis of changes in bond quality. Thus, the analysis of the proportion of bonds rated as acceptable for amortization on a cost basis is a useful measure of changes in bond quality over time.

Determining the N.A.I.C. ratings for direct placement corporate debt obligations was involved and subject to several types of error. Each direct placement issue recorded in the semiannual and annual lists compiled by the *Investment Dealers' Digest* was looked for in the annual handbook compiled by N.A.I.C. If it was found there, it was given the rating indicated ("yes" if it passed Test 1 and was therefore judged to be investment grade and "no" if below investment grade).[11] Direct placements failed to be listed or were in error if (1) no announcement was made of the offering in the *Investment Dealers' Digest,* (2) the announcement or listing was wrong or misleading, or (3) none of the placements went to an insurance company and therefore they were not graded by N.A.I.C. An idea of the total error involved in these three types of problems may be obtained by comparing columns 7 and 8 of Table A-1, which shows how this study's total of direct placements compares with those of the SEC. In some years, the total used in this study was two-thirds or less of the SEC total, probably because some of the direct placements were not officially announced. The least error probably comes from direct placements being made outside the life insurance field, although the possibility of different quality standards for direct placements taken by pension funds, investment trusts, or other institutions not subject to rigid investment supervision should not be overlooked.

Table 15 shows that direct placements rated "no" by N.A.I.C., and thus equivalent to subinvestment-grade obligations marketed to the general public, amounted to a maximum of 4.1 per cent in one year and were usually closer to 1 per cent. This is a better showing than that made by public offerings, in which the high point was 21 per cent and 4 per cent was common. This finding of the superior quality, as shown by agency ratings, of direct placements versus public offerings is not surprising, particularly when the data are confined to obligations purchased by life insurance companies, subject to rigid supervision.

The conclusions from the N.A.I.C. data depend in part on the interpretation of the standards and changes in standards used by that organization until 1953, when the present tests were adopted. Moreover, in the period after 1953 there is the real question of whether a 1.5 times earnings coverage can be considered as including bonds of quality within the first four rating grades. Finally, from 1940 through

---

[11] The designation of "yes" indicates the particular security is eligible under the rules of N.A.I.C. for valuation at cost adjusted by amortization of premium or discount at a rate sufficient to establish a 1 per cent security valuation reserve. Those designated "no" must be amortized on a 20 per cent basis and, in addition, are usually valued at a figure specified by the N.A.I.C.

TABLE 15

*Bonds Rated as Subinvestment Grade by Rating Agencies,
Public Versus Direct Offerings, 1944-65*

Year or Period of Offerings	Public Offerings (per cent rated Baa or below by Moody's)	Direct Offerings (per cent rated "no" by NAIC)
1944	2.6	.0
1945	4.4	.0
1946	3.6	.7
1947	.7	a
1948	1.0	.1
1949	2.3	1.8
1950	2.9	.5
1951	2.3	.4
1952	1.3	2.9
1953	1.1	.5
1954	4.1	.6
1955	7.7	2.1
1956	10.7	.3
1957	7.6	.3
1958	4.1	.8
1959	14.6	1.0
1960	7.9	1.0
1961	5.6	2.4
1962	3.0	2.7
1963	8.2	4.1
1964	16.6	2.1
1965	21.0	3.4
Four-year averages		
1944-47	2.8	.2
1948-51	2.1	.7
1952-55	3.5	1.5
1956-59	9.2	.6
1960-63	6.1	2.8
1964-65 (2 years only)	19.3	2.8

Source: Based on Tables B-1, B-2, and B-3. Percentages based on rated bonds only.

[a]Less than .05.

1952, bonds of the fifth rating grade could have been included if they had passed yield-spread tests. This is contrary to the practice of banking supervisors, who generally regard investment-quality bonds to be those ranked in the first four rating grades.[12] To identify amortizability standards in direct offerings with agency ratings of the first four grades in public offerings is, therefore, incorrect, but the two standards do equate if they are regarded as receiving an approved investment status by supervisory agencies.

Other Evidence

Other data on the quality of direct placements offer corroborative evidence, though they cannot be directly reconciled with the previously cited material. Two surveys of life insurance company direct placements, although limited in nature, indicate the extent of quality problems.

The first survey is of a study of direct placements made to intermediate-sized industrial companies by thirteen major life insurance companies.[13] The period covered is from 1946 to 1953, when these companies accounted for over 90 per cent of the direct placements in the life insurance industry. The loans examined were those from $100,000 to $1 million to companies with funded debt not significantly above $1 million and with assets of $10 million or below. Only loans classified in the industrial and miscellaneous group were included; loans to finance companies, loans to nonprofit institutions, oil payment loans, and very short-term loans were excluded.

Toren states that of 480 loans examined, only two, in the amount of $1,125,000 (original principal), which were made to the same borrower, had resulted in loss ($405,000). This compares with gross lending of $340 million for a loss rate of 0.12 per cent.

As of December 31, 1953, there were 363 loans in the sample, of which 351 were in good standing and fully amortizable. Twelve loans for a face amount of $3,861,850 were not amortizable, or 2.3 per cent of the $169,201,000 balance outstanding on that date. Of the non-

---

[12] See Benjamin Graham, David L. Dodd, and Sidney Cottle, *Security Analysis* (4th ed.), New York, 1962.

[13] James W. Toren, "Direct Placement Loans of Thirteen Largest Life Insurance Companies as a Postwar Solution to the Problem of Long-Term Debt-Type Financing for Intermediate Size Industrial Corporations," unpublished Ph.D. dissertation, Graduate School of Business, New York University, 1956.

amortizable loans, only three were valued at less than the face amount of the bond.[14] Toren's data show that for a distinctive group of direct placement loans of intermediate-sized business firms—firms which might be expected to be susceptible to quality problems—loss and nonamortizability conditions were relatively slight.

The second survey does not directly reveal default or loss ratios, but it does cast light on the mysterious process of contract modifications in direct placements. Earlier discussion of quality among direct placements, it will be recalled, indicated that ease of contract modification might be responsible for a deceptively low volume of defaults in this category of bonds. A survey of the modification process in direct placements by Harold K. Herzog demonstrates the typical practice in one major lending institution.[15] Herzog examined the records of a major life insurance company from 1952 through 1957. This company held 6 per cent of all life insurance company holdings of public utility and industrial bonds at the end of 1957 and directly placed issues to 208 firms during the 1952–57 period.

Herzog found that 105 of the 208 companies from 1952 to 1957 were granted 310 modifications of covenants. The covenants were of four broad categories, which included (1) terms, maturity, etc.; (2) affirmative covenants in which the borrower agreed to maintain property, books, etc.; (3) negative covenants, such as restricting debt, dividends, salaries, required working capital; and (4) legal specifications of default, modifications, indenture, trustees, and so forth. He indicated that direct placements contained many of the same covenants as public offerings, but differed from the latter primarily in the greater degree of specification and greater application of the affirmative and negative covenants.[16]

Herzog found that contract modifications were most frequently made because the borrowing company grew more rapidly than had been expected or performed more aggressively. Such cases accounted for 40 per cent of the requests for modification. Thirty-seven per cent of requests for modification were for technicalities unrelated to the course of the business, and the remaining 23 per cent were requested as a result of company difficulties of one type or another.[17]

14 *Ibid.*, p. 252.
15 Harold K. Herzog, "The Modification of Indentures and Promissory Notes Used in Direct Placement Financing," unpublished M.A. thesis, Graduate School of Business, New York University, 1959.
16 *Ibid.*, p. 8.
17 *Ibid.*, pp. 15–17.

Herzog cross-tabulates modification requests by cause of request and covenant requested to be changed. He shows requirements for modification involving some debt quality problems, i.e., those due to company difficulties, industry difficulties, inherent factors, those forced by competition and default avoidance. For the most part, the requests were for modification of debt limitations or for release of property and mortgage contracts. Extensions of maturity or changes in sinking fund requirements were relatively rare, although three of the five modifications requested "to avoid default" were for changes in these provisions.

This look at contract modifications for one lender for a few years in the total postwar period suggests that the process of modifying contracts on direct placement loans is not merely due to the staving-off of formal defaults. While nearly one-third of the requests for modifications are motivated by need to relax rigid requirements, frequently on debt limitations, only a few involve a real inability to make payments as scheduled.

III

DEFAULTS

Incidence of Defaults

It was stated earlier that Hickman's methods are used as much as possible. His study of bond defaults was limited to an examination of "straight" corporate bonds, i.e., issues with a fixed coupon and single maturity. The distinction between straight bonds with a sinking fund and serial bonds becomes fine when both types are placed directly, since direct placements constitute 46 per cent of all cash offerings in 1948–65. Table 21, on which the postwar years in Table 16 are based, includes all types of bond issues. But the earlier years shown in Table 16 are from Hickman, and accordingly are based on straight bonds only.[1]

Hickman defined default as "(1) a failure to pay interest or principal in the full contractual amount when due, or (2) an exchange or contract modification (of an issue otherwise in good standing) in which the new security received or the modified issue is worth less than par." [2] The definition had to be modified for the postwar period because of the large number of direct placements and the sparsity of information on them. The text of Moody's manuals for corporations was checked under three headings in the blue sections: bonds in default, receiverships and trusteeships, and securities of reorganized companies entitled to receive cash and/or securities. The first list gave information only on bonds with unpaid interest or principal at the time the manual went to press, but from the other two sources information on contract modifications and noncontractual exchanges was obtained, mostly for publicly offered issues. Other default data were obtained from lists

[1] For the years 1944–51 default rates have been computed for straight bonds (based on Hickman's Table A-2 in *Volume of Corporate Bond Financing*) and found to be similar to the rates for all bonds computed from Table 21.

[2] *Ibid.*, p. 182. The following acts were not considered defaults: failure to pay interest on income bonds, failure to meet sinking fund provisions, modification of sinking fund provisions, modification of working capital requirements.

TABLE 16

Average Annual Default Rates for Corporate Bonds, 1900-65
(per cent)

Date	Rate
1900-43	1.7
1900-29	1.3
1930-43	2.6
1944-65	0.1
1900-09	0.9
1910-19	2.0
1920-29	1.0
1930-39	3.2
1940-49	0.4
1950-59	0.04
1940-43	0.9
1944-49	0.1
1960-65	0.03

Source: 1900-43 (straight bonds only), Hickman, *Volume of Corporate Bond Financing,* Table 22, p. 208; 1944-65 (all bonds) Table 21 of this study.

[a]Annual rates are based on amount in good standing at beginning of year.

compiled by security analysts and from bonds of firms undergoing Chapter X proceedings.[3]

The default rates given in Table 16 are the percentages of the par amounts of bonds not in default at the beginning of a given year that went into default during the year. The rate was less than 0.1 per cent in the postwar period (1944–65) compared with 1.7 per cent in the 1900–43 period. The rate was 0.4–0.5 per cent in the decade of the

[3] See Per H. Sjogram, "Enterprise Valuation by the Securities and Exchange Commission under Chapter X of the Bankruptcy Act," unpublished Ph.D. dissertation, Columbia University, 1964.

TABLE 17

New Defaults of Corporate Bonds by
Year of Occurrence, 1944-65
(dollars in millions)

Year of Default	Straight and Serial Bonds[a]		Income Bonds		Total	
	No. (1)	Par Amount (2)	No. (3)	Par Amount (4)	No. (5)	Par Amount (6)
1944	5	34.1	1	0.4	6	34.5
1945	7	19.6	2	6.7	9	26.3
1946	4	1.7	1	0.2	5	1.9
1947	10	18.9	3	7.6	13	26.5
1948	11	33.2	7	17.9	18	51.1
1949	10	25.6	2	5.1	12	30.7
1950	3	0.8	0	0.0	3	0.8
1951	1	1.6	2	2.4	3	4.0
1952	2	1.1	3	57.2	5	58.3
1953	2	2.1	1	0.6	3	2.7
1954	2	1.9	0	0.0	2	1.9
1955	6	30.3	1	1.6	7	31.9
1956	2	3.2	0	0.0	2	3.2
1957	2	10.3	4	45.2	6	55.5
1958	6	28.7	1	1.3	7	30.0
1959	7	13.1	0	0.0	7	13.1
1960	3	7.3	0	0.0	3	7.3
1961	4	103.2	1	3.2	5	106.4
1962	1	0.5	0	0.0	1	0.5
1963	1	2.4	0	0.0	1	2.4
1964	0	0.0	0	0.0	0	0.0
1965	2	7.1	0	0.0	2	7.1
Total	91	346.7	29	149.4	120	496.1

Source: NBER compilation of data in Moody's manuals and other sources as described in text.

[a]Included are five defaults with total par amount of $16.1 million, with interest partially fixed and partially contingent on earnings. Also included are six serial bonds with par amount of $27.3 million ($.5 million in 1948, $.2 million in 1950, $25 million in 1958, $.5 million in 1959, $.5 million in 1962, and $.6 million in 1965).

forties mainly because of the somewhat higher rates in the war years, and less than 0.1 per cent in the fifties and early sixties.

Characteristics of Postwar Bond Defaults

As Table 17 shows, 120 corporate bonds with par value of $496.1 million went into default from 1944 through 1965. Of this amount, 29 issues ($149.4 million) were income bonds and 91 issues ($346.7 million) were fixed-coupon bonds (straight and serial).

The majority of the bonds defaulting in the postwar period (Table 18) were offered after 1929, although some of them were refundings of earlier issues. Forty-five issues offered after 1943, amounting to almost $200 million, defaulted. Half were industrial bonds; in fact, all but three manufacturing issues which went into default in the postwar period were also offered in the period. In terms of par amount, transportation defaults were the most important, but the New York, New Haven and Hartford Railroad accounted for over 70 per cent of the transportation total.

TABLE 18

New Defaults of Corporate Bonds in 1944-65, by Decade of Offering
(dollars in millions)

Year of Offerings	Straight and Serial Bonds[a]		Income Bonds		Total	
	No.	Amount	No.	Amount	No.	Amount
Before 1900	2	5.1			2	5.1
1900-09	12	25.5			12	25.5
1910-19	8	47.0	3	39.9	11	86.9
1920-29	12	43.4	3	16.6	15	60.0
1930-39	14	34.6	17	78.2	31	112.8
1940-49	16	96.8	4	9.4	20	106.2
1950-59	23	80.7	2	5.3	25	86.0
1960-65	4	13.6			4	13.6
Total	91	346.7	29	149.4	120	496.1

Source: Same as Table 17.

[a]Included are six serial bonds with par amount of $27.3 million ($.7 million [two issues] offered in 1940-49 and $25 million in 1950-59, $.5 million in 1959, and $1.1 million [two issues] in 1960-65).

Table 19 shows that half of the postwar default experience in terms of par amount was in the railroad (and street railway) industry. Examination of the names of defaulting railroads suggests that problems of commuter transportation, unsound management, and duplicating facilities played a role; also, certain roads run by American companies abroad were affected by governmental edicts.

TABLE 19

New Defaults of Corporate Bonds by Industry of Obligor, 1944-65
(dollars in millions)

Industry	Number	Par Amount
Transportation		
Railroad	31	$151.1
Street railways and buses	13	104.7
Airlines	1	12.0
Terminals	5	4.4
Bridges	2	0.4
Trucking	2	7.1
Total	54	279.7
Public Utilities		
Electricity[a]	10	108.1
Gas	5	3.2
Telephone	3	0.9
Warehousing	2	4.3
Water	3	3.3
Total	23	119.8
Industrials		
Manufacturing	21	63.1
Mining	12	20.6
Trade	3	2.2
Service, agriculture, construction	7	10.7
Total	43	96.6
Grand Total	120	496.1

Source: Same as Table 17.

[a]Includes companies distributing electricity and other services.

CHART 6

*Par Amount of New Defaults of Straight Bonds
by Year of Occurrence, 1900–65*

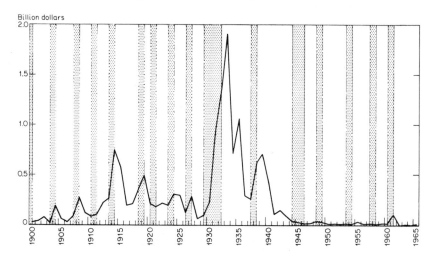

Source: 1900–43: Hickman, *Volume of Corporate Bond Financing,* Table A-17,
p. 340; 1944–65: Table 17 of this study, excluding serials mentioned in note a of
that table.

Note: Shaded areas represent business contractions; unshaded areas, expansions.

Relation of Defaults to Business Cycles

Chart 6 extends Hickman's data (through 1943) to 1965. Hickman
states that his chart shows new defaults "reaching peaks at or near
trough years in general business activity and troughs at or near peak
years." [4] In the postwar years no such clear pattern emerges. The
small number of defaults involved issues with great size variations and
were scattered throughout all years except 1964.

More interesting than the business cycle phase at which defaults
occurred is the phase at which the offerings were made. Did bonds
offered at or near the peak of business cycles default more often than
those offered at other stages of the cycle?

The greatest number and volume of defaults occurred in bonds offered one year prior to peaks, presumably a time of greatest optimism.
Table 20 shows also that the trough years were second in importance
as periods when bonds were issued which subsequently went to default.

[4] Hickman, *Volume of Corporate Bond Financing,* p. 195.

TABLE 20

*Straight and Serial Bonds Offered and Defaulted by
Stage of Reference Cycle of Offering Date, 1944-65*
(dollars in millions)

Stage of Reference Cycle	Number	Par Amount
Two years prior to peak (trough year)	5	5.4
Two years prior to peak (nontrough year)	3	11.5
One year prior to peak (nontrough year)	15	110.2
Peak year	6	16.9
One year following peak (nontrough year)	2	1.6
One year following peak (trough year)	7	30.4
Two years following trough (nonpeak year)	2	7.1
Total	40	183.1

Source: Same as Table 17.

Bonds in Default and in Good Standing

Table 21 presents estimates of the amount of outstanding corporate
bonds in default and in good standing over the period 1944–65. It
finds that bonds in default represented over 10 per cent of the total
amount outstanding in 1944–45, but had dwindled to 0.1 per cent by
the end of the period analyzed. The right-hand column of the table
shows that there was only a trickle of new defaults in the postwar
period; over a third of these defaults came under the second definition,
i.e., exchange or contract modification. In such cases default and settlement are coincident and the bond is never outstanding in default.
Most of the other postwar defaults were settled quickly.

TABLE 21

Estimated Par Amount of Outstanding Corporate Bonds by Default Status and Par Amount of New Defaults, Annually, 1944-65
(dollars in millions)

| Year | Outstanding Issues[a] | | | New Defaults[c] |
	Total[b]	In Default	In Good Standing	
1944	25,390	3,050	22,340	34.5
1945	24,660	2,530	22,130	26.3
1946	23,480	1,970	21,510	1.9
1947	24,370	1,390	22,980	26.5
1948	27,160	780	26,380	51.1
1949	31,400	790	30,610	30.7
1950	34,060	750	33,310	0.8
1951	35,590	680	34,910	4.0
1952	39,010	650	38,360	58.3
1953	43,710	610	43,100	2.7
1954	47,220	600	46,620	1.9
1955	50,760	560	50,200	31.9
1956	53,780	540	53,240	3.2
1957	57,380	160	57,220	55.5
1958	63,440	180	63,260	30.0
1959	69,090	170	68,920	13.1
1960	72,170	160	72,010	7.3
1961	75,590	120	75,470	106.4
1962	79,850	160	79,690	0.5
1963	83,880	110	83,770	2.4
1964	87,660	110	87,550	0.0
1965	91,650	100	91,550	7.1

[a]Includes serials, incomes, equipment obligations, as well as straight bonds. No equipment obligations went to default during the period.

[b]Obtained by methods shown in Hickman, *Volume of Corporate Bond Financing,* Table 26, p. 230 f. (for bonds of all types). Differences in 1950-51 from figures shown *ibid.,* Table A-1, p. 251, result from revisions in SEC figures. No adjustment was made for discrepancy between net cash flow and net change in outstandings after 1950 since the two series were assumed to be rather close in the later period.

[c]From Table 17.

IV

AGENCY RATINGS

Corporate bonds have been rated by one or more private agencies since 1909. Even direct offerings are currently rated, so that agency ratings essentially cover all corporate bonds.

The ratings ordinarily attempt to rank issues according to risk of default, although this intent is not specifically stated in the current explanation by the principal agencies. One agency refers to the attempt to grade bonds by their "relative investment quality" in the foreseeable future without regard to current or future price or yield.[1] The other is even less direct, stating that its ratings are a "simple measure of basic investment quality." It implies that although earning power is the most important criterion of analysis, as it "measures the obligor's ability to accumulate funds to pay principal and interest," [2] it is default risk that is being measured.

The rating agencies indicate that they do not assign ratings merely on the basis of statistical analysis. In general, according to the agencies currently compiling ratings, the first two grades (Aaa and Aa or AAA and AA) are high-grade bonds with neither present default risk nor foreseeable susceptibility to this kind of risk in the future. The next two grades (A and Baa or A and BBB) are considered to have some speculative characteristics in the way of possible future lack of earnings protection, but for the present are considered secure in interest and principal payments. Bonds in the Ba or BB category (fifth grade) are those which have little future assurance and only minor investment characteristics. Bonds below these five grades are speculative in character in that there can be no assurance of payment of interest or dividends. Normally, the rating agencies do not rate issues of finance companies or real estate companies whose underlying assets they are unable to evaluate.

---

[1] Moody's Investors Service, *Moody's Industrial Manual,* New York, 1964, pp. V–VI.
[2] Standard & Poor's Corporation, *Standard Corporation Descriptions,* New York, Vol. 26, No. 3, Section 4, January 29, 1965, pp. 2–3.

Hickman has demonstrated that the record of the agencies in rating bonds at offering was remarkably good from 1900 to 1943, in that highly rated issues suffered a much smaller incidence of default than did lower-rated issues. For example, for all large issues offered during the period 1900–43, only 11 per cent of the dollar volume rated as of "investment quality" (i.e., in the first four grades) went to default in those years in contrast with 42 per cent of the volume rated as "predominantly speculative." [3]

Since the postwar period lacks ex post measures, agency ratings provide perhaps the most significant indication of bond quality, even though ex ante, because they represent an assessment of many different variables affecting risk. While they cannot be taken as perfect substitutes for an economic test sufficient to produce a noticeable number of defaults, they are one of the better measures of quality currently available. Moody's ratings have been used in this study. Essentially, they rate the same sample of bonds, as Standard & Poor's, principally publicly offered issues of major corporations.

It would be incomplete to leave the topic of casualty rates among bonds classified by different agency ratings without indicating one of Hickman's findings which has been subject to later reinterpretation. Hickman found that actual loss rates did not completely eliminate the higher yields accorded bonds with lower agency ratings. Loss rates were actually negative in the first four agency rating grades (indicating a gain) and only in grades V–IX was the realized yield lower than the promised yield by reason of losses.[4] Fraine and Mills, and later Fraine alone, restudied the problem whether agency ratings are a substitute for the ultimate indicator of quality, i.e., dollar losses.[5] They eliminated call premiums obtained on better-quality bonds that did not default and high terminal prices for bonds still outstanding at the end of Hickman's period because it was one of low interest rates. Their modified loss rates were found to increase directly with a reduction in agency rating.[6]

[3] See W. Braddock Hickman, *Corporate Bond Quality and Investor Experience,* Princeton for NBER, 1958, Table 33, p. 176.

[4] *Ibid.,* Table 1, p. 10.

[5] Harold G. Fraine and Robert H. Mills, "Effect of Defaults and Credit Deterioration on Yields of Corporate Bonds," *Journal of Finance,* September 1961, and Fraine, *Valuation of Securities Holdings of Life Insurance Companies,* Homewood, Ill., 1962.

[6] Fraine, *Valuation of Securities,* p. 48.

Publicly Offered Bonds

In the period 1944–65, 93.5 per cent of all rated publicly offered straight bonds were placed in the first four rating grades. This figure, of course, excludes finance, real estate, and similar bonds; also the 1 per cent not rated. The addition of serial bonds to this tabulation does not alter essentially the finding that only 6.5 per cent in dollar terms was rated below the first four grades.

How does this finding compare with the prewar period? Tabulation of the Hickman data from 1909, when rating grades commenced, through 1943 indicates that 83 per cent of rated public offerings in that period were placed in the first four rating grades. For public offerings, therefore, the postwar quality as indicated by agency ratings was apparently better than the quality of prewar bonds as shown by this measure.

The distribution of public offerings by agency rating grades was covered earlier in the comparison of public and direct placements. The percentage of publicly offered bonds rated below the first four rating grades is given in Table 15.

"Investment Grade" Ratings of All Corporate Bonds

An over-all judgment of trends in bond quality requires a consistent measure or indicator of quality that applies to direct placements and public offerings alike. Lacking this, the analysis will be subject to speculation that shifts of bond financing from public to direct offerings, or vice versa, obscure what is happening to credit quality. Although it has not been possible to solve the problem of quality comparisons of two unlike types of bonds, it is possible to make a comparison in terms of two broad classes, investment grade and subinvestment grade bonds.

As indicated earlier, over the years there has developed a convention that certain bonds possess investment, as distinct from speculative, characteristics. For example, in 1949, the three federal bank examination agencies with a committee of the National Association of Supervisors of State Banks issued a statement of examination procedure, followed since 1938, which describes those bonds achieving favored treatment for valuation purposes: "Group I securities are marketable obligations in which the investment characteristics are not distinctly

TABLE 22

Percentage Distribution of Public Offerings and Direct Placements of Corporate Bonds Among Agency Ratings, Four-Year Periods, 1908-65

Period of Offerings	Investment Grade	Subinvestment Grade		No Rating	Total Par Amount (million dollars)
		Per Cent of Total	Per Cent of Rated		
1908-11	24.8	6.0	19.5	69.2	4,808.8
1912-15	45.5	11.0	19.5	43.5	4,942.7
1916-19	65.9	14.0	17.5	20.1	4,552.7
1920-23	79.3	17.7	18.2	3.0	7,911.0
1924-27	81.7	17.1	17.3	1.2	11,011.0
1928-31	77.8	18.8	19.5	3.4	9,963.1
1932-35	72.6	20.6	22.1	6.8	4,214.2
1936-39	85.3	11.4	11.8	3.3	9,400.9
1940-43	68.8	8.6	11.1	22.6	6,128.8
1944-47	96.4	2.3	2.3	1.3	13,975.8
1948-51	96.0	1.3	1.3	2.7	15,822.6
1952-55	95.3	2.6	2.7	2.1	22,296.9
1956-59	89.8	5.2	5.5	5.0	27,269.4
1960-63	91.9	4.4	4.6	3.7	27,653.8
1964-65[a]	86.4	9.0	9.4	4.5	16,107.9

Source: 1908-43, Hickman, *Corporate Bond Quality and Investor Experience,* Table 28, p. 153; 1944-65, Tables B-1, B-2, and B-3 of this study.

[a]Two years only.

or predominantly speculative. This group includes general market obligations in the four highest grades and unrated securities of equivalent value." [7] A similar determination of "investment grade" for insurance companies has existed since the early 1930's through ratings published by the National Association of Insurance Commissioners, although standards in terms of published rating grades have changed; only since 1951 has the favored classification been equated to the first four rating grades.

If one can conclude that the intent of the N.A.I.C. ratings was to designate "investment grade" obligations in selecting those securities

[7] *Federal Reserve Bulletin,* July 1949, p. 777.

eligible for prime treatment in valuation method, it is possible to combine public and private offerings to obtain the percentage distribution of bonds considered investment grade and below investment grade by one or another of the rating agencies.[8] Using this definition, Table 22 shows that since the 1920's [9] approximately 97 per cent of all corporate bonds have been rated, and that the percentage rated subinvestment grade fell through the beginning of the postwar period and has not varied greatly since then except for a sharp increase in the last two years. At the time of this writing, it is not possible to interpret the increase with any assurance of accuracy.

Cyclical Aspects

Hickman's analysis of the cyclical characteristics of bonds by agency ratings was made largely in terms of the net upgrading and downgrading of outstanding issues. He found that rating agencies tended to upgrade issues in the expansion phase of the business cycle and downgrade them during contractions. Our findings indicate what types of offerings are associated with different cyclical phases, but do not describe the behavior of rating agencies themselves during the cycle. The problem is, of course, that during the cycle not only may the character of bond offerings change with respect to their quality but also those analysts judging the quality of given bond issues may become more lenient or less lenient depending on their view of the business conditions that are likely to prevail over the life of the bond. The rating agencies indicate that ratings of a given issue should not be conditioned by the stage of the business cycle, but it may not be possible to prevent changes in the thinking of those who judge quality according to the business cycle.

Short of submission of a series of "sample standard" bond issues to the analysts of rating agencies over several business cycles, there is no way to determine how much the change in ratings is a psychological

---

[8] This analysis, of course, ignores an unknown but obviously small volume of bonds directly placed between 1945 and 1950 which were rated as "investment grade," i.e., eligible for preferred valuation treatment even though equivalent to public offerings rated in the fifth agency rating class (Ba or BB).

[9] The large proportion not rated in 1940–43 would probably have been reduced to that of other periods since 1920 if N.A.I.C. ratings had been used for direct offerings.

one and how much is due to a change in objective facts as these offerings reach the market at various points in the business cycle. The problem is further complicated by lack of clarity on what might be expected to happen to objective quality factors over the successive stages of the cycle. On the one hand, as an expansion progresses it might be reasoned that firms would show a stronger financial position; conversely, in a recession, they might show financial deterioration and therefore their bonds might be judged poorer risks. On the other hand, the nature of business expansion is to offer hope of success to enterprises that might not succeed except in boom periods. Similarly, investors may be receptive to poor bonds in expansion periods but wary of them in recessions. This might cause bond offerings of relatively poor quality to be brought forth during expansions, with the opposite occurring during recessions.

Chart 7 shows that, in the first two business cycle expansions of the postwar period, a smaller proportion of offerings at the peak were rated subinvestment grade than at the previous trough. In the later

CHART 7

Percentage of Rated Bond Offerings in Subinvestment Grade, 1944–65 [a]

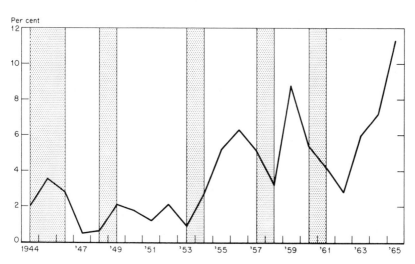

Source: Tables B-1, B-2, and B-3.
Note: Shaded areas represent business contractions; unshaded areas, expansions.
[a] Includes public offerings and direct placements of straight and serial bonds.

two recoveries (1954–57 and 1958–60) the opposite was the case. Precisely the opposite behavior was characteristic of the recession periods (eliminating 1944–46). The facts are consistent with the hypothesis that until 1954 the quality of bond offerings was primarily a function of the financial standing of companies, but that after 1954 quality varied inversely with presumed prospects, the greatest change taking place in the period following 1962.

Another facet of the problem should be considered. Less than 12 per cent of offerings (by value) received a subinvestment grade rating in any year of the period 1944–65; hence the division into two groups may be too gross to show adequately the sensitivity to business cycles. More marked cyclical conformity might appear in the proportion in a larger class, such as the third grade or below.

Following this approach, the data on postwar cyclical swings in agency ratings are shown in Chart 8 only for public offerings of straight bonds, since the agency ratings on direct placements (N.A.I.C.) do not make a fine enough distinction for private offerings. The bottom curve represents what previously has been called "subinvestment grade" (grade V and below), but it differs slightly from Chart 7 because of differences in underlying data. The next higher curve represents grade IV and below, and so on. The spaces between the curves represent individual rating grades.

For public offerings of straight bonds, the class grade V and below has comprised from less than 1 to 21 per cent of rated public offerings in various postwar years. If only the first three grades are considered "investment grade," then "subinvestment grade" (grade IV and below) has represented 5 to 37 per cent. That curve rises in four of the five contractions. The same is true of grade II and below, while the intermediate curve (grade III and below) rises in only three contractions. The chart is hard to interpret, but it does show clearly the following three points:

1. The proportion of prime bonds (grade I–Aaa) increased from a low point (5 per cent) in 1952,[10] but since the early 1960's has been shrinking.

---

[10] This is exaggerated in 1960–63 by the upgrading of American Telephone and Telegraph bonds. If new offerings by that company had been rated only Aa in 1960–63, as in earlier years, grade I would have amounted to the following percentages of total rated offerings: 1960, 24.1; 1961, 13.3; 1962, 15.9; 1963, 19.4.

CHART 8

*Percentage Distribution of Public Offerings of Straight Bonds
by Rating Grade, Annually, 1944–65* ª

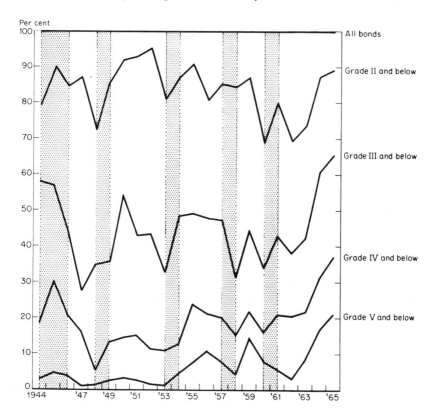

Source: Computed from Table B-1.
Note: Shaded areas represent business contractions; unshaded areas, expansions.
ª Based on rated bonds only.

2. On the average, just over half of the dollar volume of rated bonds were during the period in grades I or II and just under half in grade III and below. This is not true in the last two years.

3. The curve for grade III and below reached its highest point of the postwar period in 1965.

V

EARNINGS COVERAGE

Of prime importance in the quality of a corporate bond is the ability of the issuing firm to pay interest charges on the debt out of income produced. Thus, the level, trend, and stability of corporate income in relation to interest and other fixed charges are basic to the assignment of ratings by the rating agencies. In practice, the means of measuring this characteristic has been the so-called earnings coverage, or ratio of earnings to fixed charges. Such a ratio averaged for a period of a few years prior to issue gives an impression of the level of possible income relative to debt charges, though not of trend and stability of earnings.

Hickman found that whereas 17 per cent of all large issues in the period from 1900 to 1943 defaulted at some time before 1944, 35 per cent of those with average earnings of less than the *pro forma* fixed charges in the five years preceding offering went to default. In contrast, only 2 per cent (of the par amount of bond issues) with past earnings equal to three or more times *pro forma* fixed charges went to default.[1]

Hickman's estimates were obtained by dividing the average earnings of the issuing corporation for the five years preceding offering by the fixed charges in the year following offering. Because of inadequate data in the early manuals, all taxes including income taxes were deducted from earnings (i.e., the ratios were after tax). Included as fixed charges were all interest on funded and unfunded debt, rentals and amortization of debt discount, and preferred dividends of subsidiaries.

Moody's *Bond Survey,* the source of the postwar data on public offerings, contains single-year before-tax ratios for years preceding offering based on *pro forma* charges at offering. The denominator usually includes only interest on debt with one year or longer to maturity; but when rents or other fixed charges are larger, two sets of ratios are shown, one for interest only and one for interest and other charges. In this study the latter ratios were used when published. Annual ratios for the five years preceding offering were averaged.

To make the two series comparable, Hickman's data were converted

[1] See W. Braddock Hickman, *Corporate Bond Quality and Investor Experience,* Princeton for NBER, 1958, Table 1, p. 10.

to a before-tax basis by a series of factors compiled from *Statistics of Income* data for nonfinancial corporations. The difference between before- and after-tax ratios only becomes visible in 1918.

Inclusion of fixed charges other than interest as a part of the annual expense necessary to be covered by earnings is particularly important in the postwar period, when many companies found it advantageous from a tax viewpoint to lease facilities. In effect, they exchanged an interest charge for a rent charge.

CHART 9

Times Charges Earned Before Taxes, Bond-Issuing Corporations Compared with All U.S. Nonfinancial Corporations, 1900–62

Source: Bond-issuing corporations: Chart 1; all nonfinancial corporations: computed from *Statistics of Income.* For comparison with bond-issuing corporations compiled net income plus interest and rent paid averaged for five years preceding date plotted divided by interest and rent paid in year following date plotted. See Hickman, *Corporate Bond Quality and Investor Experience,* p. 395.

Following the plan of previous chapters, the long-term trend of the times-charges-earned ratio will be analyzed over four-year periods and then for each year to discover the influence of the business cycle. Our source of postwar direct placements did not include fixed-charge coverage, but we were able to combine Cohan's direct placement data for the years 1951–61 with our public offerings data in certain tables and charts. The data in Chart 9, for example, include direct placements for all years shown, but have a gap for the years 1944–50 and 1962–65.

Hickman's data include cash and noncash offerings, whereas the postwar data include only cash offerings. Since in the postwar period the mean ratios would be distorted by extreme values, the charts and

TABLE 23

Median Times-Charges-Earned Ratio Before Taxes, Public Offerings, Four-Year Periods of Offerings, 1900-65

Year	Ratio
1900-03	1.3
1904-07	1.3
1908-11	1.5
1912-15	1.7
1916-19	1.6
1920-23	1.7
1924-27	2.0
1928-31	2.1
1932-35	2.6
1936-39	2.6
1940-43	3.5
1944-47	6.5
1948-51	4.8
1952-55	5.5
1956-59	5.6
1960-63	5.2
1964-65[a]	3.9

Source: 1900-43 (straight offerings): computed from Hickman, *Statistical Measures,* Table 79, p. 125, less special tabulations on direct offerings converted to before-tax basis (see chart 1, note 3); 1944-65 (straight and serial offerings): computed from Table C-1.

[a]The period 1964-65 covers only two years.

TABLE 24

Median Times-Charges-Earned Ratio Before Taxes,
Public Offerings, Annually, 1944-65

Year	Ratio	Year	Ratio
1944	5.3	1955	6.3
1945	6.3	1956	6.6
1946	8.1	1957	5.6
1947	5.9	1958	5.7
1948	5.7	1959	4.9
1949	4.5	1960	5.1
1950	4.5	1961	5.3
1951	4.3	1962	5.2
1952	4.9	1963	5.0
1953	5.5	1964	4.1
1954	5.0	1965	3.8

Source: Computed from Table C-1.

all tables on earnings coverage except Table 25 are in terms of medians.

Table 23 shows a practically continuous rise in earnings coverage of public offerings from 1900–03 to 1944–47, then a decline to approximately the level of 1940–43. Chart 9, which presents combined public and direct offerings, suggests that there was a smooth, slightly upward trend from the turn of the century through the early forties. Data are not available for 1944–50, but those for 1951–61 show a slight downward trend. The peak may have occurred in the omitted period or in 1952. For public offerings only (Table 24), the peak occurred in 1946.

The dip in the earnings coverage ratio for corporations with new offerings in the 1950's agrees with the downward trend in the ratio for all nonfinancial business computed from *Statistics of Income* data and also shown in Chart 9. Since the early 1950's generally, bond-issuing corporations seem to have held their earnings coverage better than all nonfinancial corporations.

Hickman has pointed out that there is a slight tendency for the market to accept bonds of lower quality, as measured by the times-charges-earned ratio, in peak years of the business cycle.[2] Such a

[2] *Ibid.,* p. 409.

CHART 10

*Earnings Coverage of Public and Direct Offerings Before Taxes,
by Industrial Group, 1944–65*

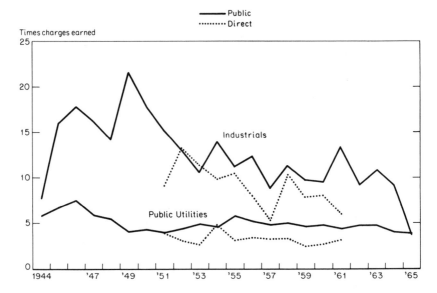

Source: Special tabulations of NBER. Data on direct offerings are from Chart 4.

tendency does not seem to have existed in the postwar period. The times-charges-earned ratio for all publicly offered corporate bonds fell from 1946–48 and from 1958–60. In 1949–53 the ratio fell and then rose; in 1954–57 it rose and then fell.

More significantly, the times-charges-earned ratio showed a broad gradual improvement over the course of the 1920's,[3] notwithstanding the cyclical action noted above. As Hickman pointed out, this was "largely a statistical mirage" caused by changes in the industrial mix. "The all-industries averages of the computed times-charges-earned ratios drifted upward as rail bonds declined in importance in total bond offerings and as more information became available for utilities and industrials." [4] The chart therefore gives no indication of whether or not the 1920's witnessed a general deterioration in quality of bond offerings. It also raises the question of how much comfort can be derived from the improvement in the times-charges-earned ratio in

[3] See Chart 9.
[4] See *ibid.*, p. 390.

case a severe test arises in the form of a major depression. In the post-war period, data were available for the majority of bond offerings, and Chart 10 shows the ratios for public offerings separately for industrial and public utility corporations. (Railroad offerings have been omitted since few were issued in that period.) The trend is downward for both industry groups. This agrees with Chart 8, which shows an increasing trend in the proportion of public offerings rated subinvestment quality.

Direct Placements—The "Slippage" Problem

Most of the data on postwar earnings coverage up to this point have referred solely to public offerings. It may be argued, however, that, with the expansion of direct placements in the postwar period, analysis of any quality measure for public offerings alone may miss a "slippage"

TABLE 25

Percentage Distribution of Public and Direct Offerings by Earnings Coverage Classes, 1900-43

Times-Charges-Earned Classes[a]	Public Offerings	Direct Offerings
Negative	1.6	—
0.0—0.9	10.4	2.1
1.0—1.4	22.3	5.5
1.5—1.9	19.1	12.9
2.0—2.4	12.7	11.8
2.5—2.9	9.9	14.2
3.0—3.9	11.1	19.3
4.0—4.9	5.8	12.5
5.0—5.9	2.6	6.7
6.0 and over	4.4	15.1
Total	99.9	100.1
Median	1.9	3.2

Source: From data compiled by Corporate Bond Research Project, on file at NBER; and Hickman, *Statistical Measures of Corporate Bond Financing,* Table 79, p. 125.

Note: Offerings for which times-charges-earned could not be computed have been omitted from this table.

[a]After taxes.

of bonds of a particular quality category out of the public offering market and into the direct placement field. Obviously, it could be concluded that no quality deterioration of public offerings had taken place, while significant deterioration actually had occurred in the total bond population as a large volume of poor-quality bonds were offered outside of public channels in the form of direct placements. Table 25 compares, for 1900–43, earnings coverage ratios for public offerings and for direct offerings. For that entire period, public offerings were covered approximately twice and direct offerings about three times in terms of earnings over fixed charges. This suggests that the quality of direct placements was better than public offerings in the period prior to this study.

What has happened to earnings coverage of direct placements versus public offerings in the postwar period? From Avery Cohan's sample of direct placements held by selected lending institutions, principally life insurance companies, it is possible to obtain medians of the times-charges-earned ratio. Chart 10 and Table 26 show that in the postwar period direct placements had appreciably lower earnings coverage than public offerings in the same industry groups. The development of direct placements may have provided a slippage of poor-quality bonds into this less easily observed category. It is interesting to note that, for the two postwar groups of years analyzable from Cohan's data, both public and direct placement offerings declined in earnings coverage ratios (except for the publicly placed utilities).

TABLE 26

Comparison of Times Charges Earned Before Taxes for Public Offerings and a Sample of Direct Placements, 1951-61
(medians)

Period of Offerings	Direct Placements[a]		Public Offerings[b]	
	Industrials	Utilities	Industrials	Utilities
1951-55	9.7	3.1	12.0	4.5
1956-61	7.5	2.9	10.9	4.7

[a]Computed in terms of par amount of offerings from data of Avery Cohan.

[b]Computed from Moody's *Bond Survey*.

Earnings coverage is measured by the number of times interest and other fixed charges are covered by the income of the bond-issuing corporation. While this concept is basic to bond analysis and there is a considerable correlation between bond defaults and low earnings coverage ratios, the aggregate measure for all bond-issuing corporations has not been useful in foretelling periods of high defaults. For example, the 1920's saw generally rising earnings coverage for bond-issuing corporations, and the median times-charges-earned continued to rise through World War II and into the early postwar years.

Coverage for the publicly offered bonds which could be analyzed reached a peak in 1946, receded, recovered in 1955–56, and has drifted gently downward since. The level of earnings coverage for bond-issuing corporations still remains close to the prewar highs, and there is no reason to believe the secular drift toward higher earnings coverage has ceased.

For the years available since the mid-thirties, bond-issuing corporations as a group have shown greater earnings coverage than all nonfinancial corporations. These findings suggest that the "quality problem" in corporate indebtedness is largely one of non-bond-issuing smaller corporations. By implication it would also seem to be a problem of banks, since this is the principal source of external business funds not supplied through bond issues. As for the relation of earnings coverage to business cycles, the modest inverse conformity that Hickman found for the prewar period has not reappeared since the war.

The evidence indicates that postwar earnings coverage of direct offerings is poorer than that of public offerings; but when all industry groups are combined, the large proportion of industrials among direct offerings camouflages this fact. This suggests that some poorer-quality bonds were simply disappearing by taking the form of directly placed issues and, as a result, that observation of public offerings alone is misleading. In addition, for the two groups of postwar years for which comparison of earnings coverage for public and direct bonds has been possible, the quality deterioration of direct placements of industrial bonds is relatively greater. Even so, earnings coverage of direct placements in the postwar period is extremely high compared with historical standards.

VI

LIEN POSITION AND
MARKET RATING

Two indicators of credit quality have been found to be associated with the ultimate success or failure of bond investments, namely, agency ratings and earnings coverage. This chapter considers two other quality indicators of corporate bonds: lien position and market rating. Lien position refers to whether or not the debt is secured; market rating, to how the market itself rates the bond.

Lien Position

A principal lesson of the 1930's to the bond investor was that the presence of specific security or the manner in which a debt obligation was secured had little to do with whether or not it ultimately went to default. Indeed, Hickman's study of the period from 1900 to 1943 showed that security was inversely related to earnings; that is, companies with low earnings coverage offered a greater proportion of secured issues. Thus, earnings and the security provision could be considered substitutes to a degree.[1]

In much of the period Hickman was analyzing, unsecured and junior obligations suffered relatively fewer defaults than did senior and secured obligations, because only strong corporations were able to finance with debentures, except in periods of excessive optimism.[2] Among defaulting bonds, however, security and rank of claims had a large bearing on the loss rate. For example, while 18.8 per cent of large secured issues went into default (compared with 13.6 per cent unsecured), the loss rate was only 8.0 per cent (compared with 16.6 per cent unsecured).[3] When both the possibility of default and of loss resulting from default are considered, the difference between large secured and unsecured issues is not great. On all large issues (nondefaulted plus defaulted), 5.4 per cent was realized on secured and

---

[1] See W. Braddock Hickman, *Corporate Bond Quality and Investor Experience,* Princeton for NBER, 1958, p. 392 ff.

[2] *Ibid.,* pp. 447 ff.

[3] *Ibid.,* Tables 93 and 97, pp. 448 and 462.

TABLE 27

Lien Position of Public and Direct Offerings 1944-65
(percentage of offerings secured and unsecured)

Period of Offerings	Secured	Unsecured
1900-03	95.7	4.3
1904-07	77.8	22.2
1908-11	82.0	18.0
1912-15	77.6	22.4
1916-19	81.6	18.4
1920-23	72.7	27.3
1924-27	71.6	28.4
1928-31	55.4	44.6
1932-35	80.4	19.6
1936-39	67.5	32.5
1940-43	67.4	32.6
1944-47	56.9	43.1
1948-51	47.1	52.9
1952-55	41.2	58.8
1956-59	41.3	58.7
1960-63	37.6	62.4
1964-65	36.2	63.8

Source: 1900-43: Hickman, *Corporate Bond Quality and Investor Experience,* Table 91, p. 437; 1944-65: tabulations from Table D-1.

5.3 per cent on unsecured obligations.[4] Hickman concluded that while protection of both earnings and assets was generally rewarded by lower defaults, large institutional investors could substitute earnings coverage for lien position and obtain a high average realized yield.[5]

Table 27 shows that there has been a much lower proportion of secured offerings in the postwar period than prevailed in the prewar period, particularly the decade immediately prior to the war. For the 1900–43 period, about 73 per cent of the bond offerings were secured. In contrast, the postwar average is about 42 per cent of offerings secured.

[4] *Ibid.,* Table 98, p. 466.
[5] *Ibid.,* p. 469.

CHART 11

Proportion of Offerings Secured, 1900–65

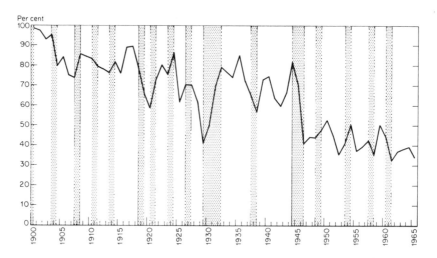

Source: Computed from Hickman, *Statistical Measures of Corporate Bond Financing*, Table 85, and Table D-1 of this study.

Note: Shaded areas represent business contractions; unshaded areas, expansions.

Hickman found that the proportion of unsecured obligations to total bond offerings rose toward the end of the 1920's, mainly because of financing by holding companies with no mortgageable assets.[6] While there has been no comparable holding-company movement in the postwar period, it may be worthwhile to study the trend of secured versus unsecured issues, if only to determine whether the tolerance of the market for unsecured offerings may be a symptom of deterioration in credit quality.

Chart 11 indicates that in the prewar period business recoveries often were characterized by a declining proportion of offerings that bore specific security. The most notable example was the fall, prior to the 1929 turning point, in percentage of offerings secured. In the postwar period a slight tendency continued for recoveries to show a falling proportion of secured offerings. However, the long secular downdrift from 1900 to 1929 was no longer present in the postwar period; the proportion of secured offerings leveled off at 40 per cent in 1946.

[6] *Ibid.*, pp. 435, 449.

Hickman found that lien position at offering had little to do with the risk of occurrence of default; in fact, the reverse seemed to be the case sometimes, since weak corporations could only finance by offering secured issues. Instead, past differences in ability to meet charges seemed to have the greatest relation to incidence of default. On the other hand, the security of the bond became important in determining the amount of the loss when and if the bond went into default.[7]

Market Rating

A measure of risk in corporate bonds is afforded by the evaluation placed upon them by investors. Presumably, a bond which the market judges to have a minimum risk will be bid up to the point where its yield equals the "pure" cost of long-term money plus an amount sufficient only to cover the most remote chance of loss from default. Similarly, a bond judged by the market to have a high degree of risk should afford additional return beyond the pure cost of long-term funds, this additional compensation being a measure of the market appraisal of the chances of possible loss.

Hickman points out that risks on low-grade bonds were apparently overcompensated in the 1900–43 period, so that an investor able to diversify sufficiently received more than enough from the higher yields on low-quality bonds to compensate for losses incurred. He suggests that the observed facts are consistent with two hypotheses: First, the yield on a bond consists of three elements—the pure cost of money, a risk premium sufficient on the average to compensate for losses, and a reward for bearing risk. Second, although the institutions which have dominated the market in recent years can diversify adequately, they generally choose high-grade bonds because of public regulation and to avoid the embarrassment of large holdings of defaulted bonds. Promised yields on low-grade bonds are thereby more than sufficient to offset default losses.[8]

Of course, Hickman found that the degree of overcompensation for losses varied with the quality of the bond. For example, whereas bonds with the highest agency rating promised 4.5 per cent, their realized yield was actually 5.1 per cent. Only in the subinvestment-grade bonds

[7] *Ibid.*, Table 97, p. 462.
[8] *Ibid.*, pp. 15–16 and 322–324.

TABLE 28

*Life-Span Default Rates, Yields and Loss Rates for Bonds
Classified by Agency Rating, 1900-43*
(per cent)

Agency Rating	Default Rate	Promised Yield	Realized Yield	Loss Rate
I	5.9	4.5	5.1	−0.6
II	6.0	4.6	5.0	−0.4
III	13.4	4.9	5.0	−0.1
IV	19.1	5.4	5.7	−0.3
V-IX	42.4	9.5	8.6	0.9
No rating	28.6	4.8	4.6	0.2
Total	17.3	5.3	5.4	−0.1

Source: Hickman, *Corporate Bond Quality and Investor Experience*,
Table 1, p. 10.

was there a reduction from promised yield as a result of losses. Table 28 summarizes these findings.

Hickman's findings that yields on less than prime-quality bonds greatly overcompensate for the calculation of risks involved has recently been re-examined with the aim of eliminating the effect of calls and high terminal valuations in 1944, a low interest rate year, from realized yields. Table 29 shows that the modified loss rate (difference between promised and modified realized yield) is much greater for lower grades vis-à-vis high-grade bonds. Promised yields, as reflected in the "market rating" placed on bonds, hence measure bond quality.

Many factors not related to quality also affect the promised yield, among them term to maturity. Bonds convertible into common stock offer something more than the promised return on comparable non-convertible bonds, and therefore command yields often not fully commensurate with the risk of default. Particularly in times of optimism, convertible bonds may be valued as common stock. Similarly, variations in call features can affect the prospect of the bond's life and, therefore, the potentiality of the holder's realizing a capital gain with changes in interest rates. (All of this would affect investors' appraisals.) The size of the issue and the volume of outstanding debt of the particular firm

TABLE 29

Yield Experience on Corporate Bonds as Determined by Hickman and as Modified by Fraine and Mills, Distributed by Agency Rating, 1900-43

(per cent)

Agency Rating	Promised Yield	Realized Yield	
		Unmodified (Hickman)	Modified (Fraine and Mills)
I	4.5	5.1	4.3
II	4.5	5.1	4.3
III	4.9	5.0	4.3
IV	5.4	5.8	4.5
V	6.3	4.1	3.5
VI-IX	7.6	4.7	3.7
All rated bonds	5.0	5.1	4.3

Source: Harold G. Fraine and Robert H. Mills, "Effect of Defaults and Credit Deterioration on Yields of Corporate Bonds," *Journal of Finance*, September 1961, p. 431.

or industry can affect investors' appraisals. Their normal diversification requirements may make particular issues more or less attractive than others. Thus, utility bonds often have a larger yield than equally good industrial bonds simply because institutional investors have heavy portfolios of utility issues which, during most of the postwar period, have been in ample supply.

In periods of high interest rates, bonds with low coupons sell at a deep discount from par, but often are priced to yield less than bonds selling nearer to par, because investors prefer capital gains rather than current yield and expect the interest rate cycle to reverse. Also, an active sinking fund may contribute to yield differences not commensurate with quality by creating a shortage in the particular issue.

Despite the difficulties in considering the spread from prime bonds as a measure of quality, there are good reasons to treat this measure with some respect. Valuation of bonds requires a considerable body of techniques that have been developed over many years. Unlike stocks—where growth-of-earnings possibilities, dividends, and liquidating value intrude into the valuation formula—bond valuation, apart from the strict mathematical relationships, is heavily influenced by the one major event that can occur to the instrument, namely, default. Consequently, slight gradations in price and therefore yield reflect market estimates of, among other things, bond quality.

The means used here to determine the yield on best-grade corporate bonds was developed by Durand.[9] It includes plotting yields against maturity for a large number of high-grade bonds. A line is drawn representing the lower margin of yields for the sample, disregarding a few issues with very low yields because of extraneous influences. After determining the schedule of yields for each maturity, a measure of the market rating for any given issue may be obtained by subtracting the appropriate basic yield from the issue's yield. Generally, in this study, Hickman's practice of classifying bonds with yields at offering of less than 1 per cent above the basic corporate bond yield as high grade is followed. Those selling at 1 per cent or more above the basic yield are considered substandard risks.

Another difficulty with a measure of market rating representing the difference between prime bonds and a specified bond is that at different periods "the market" has valued the same quality bonds differently. This is most commonly seen in the so-called confidence index familiar to stock investors. The measure, the ratio of Aaa to Baa bond yields, is shown in Chart 12. While it is affected by Hickman's finding that the agencies during the period 1914–43 "rated bonds up in expansions and down in contractions," [10] most of its movement is a change in public valuation of different grades of bonds. As a result, the ratio varied from .54 in 1932 to .92 in 1965. The reduction in difference in Aaa and Baa yields (curve moving up) is one aspect of the finding that market ratings have improved over the period since 1919. It does not explain the 1954–60 dip and recovery.

Because of the multiplicity of yields necessary for serial bonds, yields, and therefore market ratings, were computed only for straight bonds in the early period. In the postwar data, practically all direct placements had some form of repayment arrangement similar to, if not exactly the same, as that of serial bonds.

Table 30 shows that the early postwar period improved substantially

[9] David Durand, *Basic Yields of Corporate Bonds, 1900–1942,* New York, National Bureau of Economic Research, 1942.
[10] *Corporate Bond Quality,* pp. 173 f.

CHART 12

*Percentage of Offerings with High-Grade Market Ratings Related
to Changes in Quality Premium, 1919–65* [a]

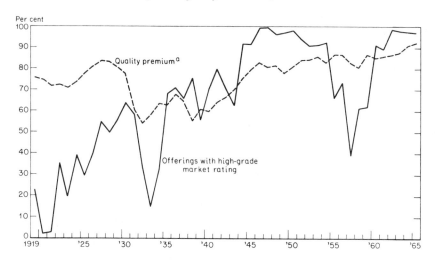

Source: Based on Hickman, *Statistical Measures of Corporate Bond Financing,*
Table 70, p. 113; Table E-1 of this study; and Moody's bond yields by rating
groups. (All corporate bonds, annual averages from blue section of Moody's *Industrial Manual.*)

[a] Ratio of yields on Aaa bonds to those on Baa bonds, annual averages of
monthly indexes.

over the prewar period in the percentage of par amount of bond offerings rated by the market as high grade, i.e., with a yield less than 1 per
cent above that of the basic yield in the year offered. There was some
deterioration in the late fifties, and quality by this measure was about
back to that of the period 1928–31. Then it rose again and was higher
in 1964–65 than in any of the four-year periods. The percentage of
bonds rated high grade would differ somewhat if, instead of constant
differential (1 per cent), a constant ratio of differential to basic rate
were used, but there would still be a larger proportion of high grades
in all postwar years except 1956–59 than in years before 1944.

Hickman, using outstandings and "net upgradings," found little
cyclical behavior in the market rating. In the postwar period, virtually
no discernible cyclical behavior is present for public offerings. While
the whole period is sharply dominated by the 1954–57 dip and subsequent recovery in the new-issue volume rated as high grade (offering

TABLE 30

Percentage Distribution of Par Amount of Straight Corporate Bond Offerings Among High and Low Market Ratings at Offering, Four-Year Periods, 1900-65

Period of Offerings	High Grade	Low Grade
1900-03	43.1	56.9
1904-07	41.9	58.1
1908-11	42.9	57.1
1912-15	43.5	56.5
1916-19	23.2	76.8
1920-23	16.3	83.7
1924-27	43.0	57.0
1928-31	56.8	43.2
1932-35	51.5	48.5
1936-39	67.2	32.8
1940-43	72.3	27.7
1944-47	95.2	4.8
1948-51	96.1	3.9
1952-55	85.3	14.7
1956-59	57.2	42.8
1960-63	94.1	5.9
1964-65[a]	97.3	2.7

Source: 1900-43; based on Hickman, *Corporate Bond Quality and Investor Experience,* Table 54, p. 298; 1944-65: based on Table E-1.

Note: High-grade issues are those with offering yields less than 100 basis points in excess of the basic yield. Beginning in 1944 only public offerings are included. Based on rated bonds only.

[a]Two-year period.

yield less than one percentage point above basic yield), there is a very modest tendency for a greater proportion of issues to be rated good in recession years than in the previous peak years. In general, however, the cyclical performance of the market rating is subordinate to obviously stronger secular movements.

The market rating probably has lost much of the efficiency as a quality indicator that it exhibited in the earlier Hickman period because such a great proportion of the dollar volume of bond issues now escapes the market process, even though market alternatives are not without influence. It has been particularly poor in the postwar period because of the rise of convertible issues. The market rating is a generally poor indicator of quality since it is affected by many influences not related to quality. Nevertheless, the results of our market rating analysis corroborates other indications that in the postwar period quality is better than prewar. The search for earnings in the last several years, however, has driven down yields on even poorer-quality bonds (as measured by other criteria), so that it is likely spurious indications of the recent trend in quality are obtained from the use of the market rating.

VII
CONVERTIBLE BONDS

The rise in convertible bond offerings has been a striking development of postwar bond financing. In part this was a natural development since it was virtually the only way in which equity investments could be sold to a market largely institutional in nature. The largest user of convertible bond issues by far has been the American Telephone and Telegraph Company. While the convertible feature is not new, as will be seen, its popularity in the postwar period is probably the result of a special need for equity funds by a few major corporations and, until the late 1950's, when pension-fund stock purchasing began in volume, lack of any institutional source of equity money. The rising stock market throughout most of the postwar period made convertibles the cheapest method of external financing for many corporations.

Ordinarily, convertible bonds have been issued as debentures. There is generally a schedule of prices at which the bond is convertible at different times. The investor receives both the protection of the bond and the opportunity to share in a rise in value of the common stock. The issuing corporation, on the other hand, is able to raise capital at moderate interest cost, and if the company prospers the issuing corporation will find its fixed income obligations eliminated automatically as holders exchange them for common stock.

Investment textbooks until recently were unfavorably disposed toward these issues, the conversion feature of which was interpreted as a substitute for quality. Indeed, a well-known text had the following advice to give on convertible issues: ". . . investors should approach these offerings with an eye for a possible Trojan horse." [1]

While there is no precise rule for valuing convertible bonds, many investors determine their attractiveness according to how much premium is paid over comparable fixed-income securities without the conversion feature. This is one important reason why the so-called

[1] Benjamin Graham and David L. Dodd, *Security Analysis*, 3rd ed., New York, 1951, p. 523.

market rating fails to give a significant indication of corporate bond quality per se in the postwar period. However, the majority of postwar investors in convertible bonds have not been so prudent as to test their value as a fixed-income security. Instead, as the bull market of the late 1950's continued to gather steam, convertible bonds became increasingly popular with investors and with corporations needing capital funds.

Why are convertible bonds possibly of greater risk than other bonds? The convertible feature of itself does not worsen the quality of a fixed-income security. So long as conversion is at the privilege of the bondholder, there is no reason why a convertible bond is any more risky than a nonconvertible bond. Rather, other attributes of the fixed-income obligation, attributes frequently closely associated with the convertibility feature, may induce added risk. In the first place, convertible bonds may be sold by corporations unable to market regular bond issues. Second, convertible bonds are nearly always unsecured by any but the general credit of the corporation and are often subordinate to other debt. In case of default, this may mean a poorer settlement. Finally, more often than not, speculative demand for convertible bonds may induce purchasers to pay more than is warranted by the risks involved. In the postwar period, convertible bonds have been a particularly favored instrument for equity-type speculation since stock margin requirements do not apply to them.

The Prewar Experience

The prevalence of convertible issues in the late postwar period suggests that it might be appropriate to examine their earlier record. How did bonds convertible into common stocks make out in the early 1930's? [2] How were they judged at the time of their offering, and how did these judgments work out in time of general defaults? The history of the 1920's and 1930's may offer insights about the effect of convertible issues on aggregate bond quality.

Table 31 shows that convertibles were some 10 per cent of the volume of straight corporate bond financing during the 1900–43 period. The peak was in 1929, when they accounted for 40 per cent of all straight

[2] A few convertible bonds issued prior to World War II were convertible into preferred stock or other classes of bonds. These have been excluded from the present study.

TABLE 31

Amount and Proportion of All Offerings of Bonds
Convertible into Common Stock, 1900-65
(dollars in millions)

Year of Offerings	Con-vertible	All	Per Cent	Year of Offerings	Con-vertible	All	Per Cent
1900	11.2	693.4	1.6	1933	39.8	444.3	9.0
1901	125.0	1489.0	8.4	1934	129.1	581.3	22.2
1902	65.6	1009.8	6.5	1935	115.8	2314.9	5.0
1903	32.6	919.2	3.5	1936	142.7	3666.1	3.9
1904	33.1	1092.0	3.0	1937	257.3	1561.6	16.5
1905	164.5	1226.0	13.4	1938	218.9	1960.1	11.2
1906	184.3	1092.0	16.9	1939	260.6	2213.1	11.8
1907	166.6	1089.3	15.3	1940	11.5	2416.4	0.5
1908	106.5	1112.1	9.6	1941	256.1	2005.2	12.8
1909	198.4	1264.0	15.7	1942	46.3	897.7	5.2
1910	123.5	1133.2	10.9	1943	0.0	809.5	0.0
1911	29.1	1299.5	2.2	1944	34.2	2194.3	1.6
1912	74.3	1396.9	5.3	1945	13.0	4245.3	0.3
1913	218.7	1167.6	18.7	1946	401.9	3810.3	10.5
1914	75.3	1193.4	6.3	1947	396.6	3725.9	10.6
1915	198.9	1184.8	16.8	1948	230.4	4064.8	5.7
1916	193.5	1485.0	13.0	1949	428.4	3490.2	12.3
1917	68.4	1228.6	5.6	1950	122.6	3730.7	3.3
1918	111.2	800.4	13.9	1951	472.8	4536.9	10.4
1919	141.9	1038.7	13.7	1952	908.9	5970.6	15.2
1920	275.0	1448.0	19.0	1953	949.3	4998.5	19.0
1921	102.0	2074.6	4.9	1954	133.9	6049.2	2.2
1922	148.1	2270.2	6.5	1955	1412.1	5278.6	26.8
1923	134.6	2118.2	6.4	1956	757.6	5987.1	12.7
1924	79.4	2227.0	3.6	1957	1056.7	7972.9	13.3
1925	159.8	2202.4	7.3	1958	1115.4	7965.7	14.0
1926	186.4	2724.8	6.8	1959	618.5	5343.7	11.6
1927	156.8	3856.8	4.1	1960	358.5	5602.0	6.4
1928	294.3	2997.0	9.8	1961	525.7	7154.9	7.3
1929	788.5	1957.7	40.3	1962	301.5	7201.3	4.2
1930	570.4	2978.3	19.2	1963	280.9	7695.6	3.7
1931	58.5	2030.1	2.9	1964	352.7	7145.0	4.9
1932	30.6	873.7	3.5	1965	888.9	8962.9	9.9

Source: 1900-43: Hickman, *Statistical Measures of Corporate Bond Financing*, Tables 70 and 118; 1944-65: Tables D-1 and F-1.

offerings. Our figures for the postwar period indicate that convertibles have also comprised about 10 per cent of all corporate debt offerings, or 16 per cent of public offerings. The peak was in 1955, with $1.4 billion in debt issues representing 27 per cent of total marketing of bonds. (The corresponding figures for public offerings are $1.3 billion and 46 per cent.)

In the 1920's and 1930's, the proportion of convertibles going into default was twice that for all corporate bonds, and this relationship apparently did not change between the two decades analyzed (Table 32).

Table 33 and Chart 13 show default rates for convertibles and for all bonds by year of offering. Since the number of convertible issues was relatively small in many years, default rates would be expected to vary more on them than on nonconvertible bonds. The chart shows a tendency for the years that produced high-grade convertible bonds to produce low-grade nonconvertibles and vice versa. The proportion of bond offerings with convertible privileges is also shown on the chart. In general, years that produced a high proportion of convertibles ultimately going to default were those years when convertibles were relatively scarce. This suggests that the high volume of convertibles issued in the postwar period does not in itself mean an increased incidence of convertible bond defaults.

May convertible bonds be rated as to likelihood of default as efficiently as others? A look at the proportion of convertibles classified as poor risk according to agency ratings, times-charges-earned, market

TABLE 32

Average Annual Default Rates, All Corporate Bonds and Convertible Bonds Outstanding, 1920-39
(per cent)

Period of Defaults	All Bonds	Convertible Bonds
1920-29	1.0	2.2
1930-39	3.2	6.3

Source: All bonds from Hickman, *Volume of Corporate Bond Financing,* Table 22, p. 208; convertibles computed from data compiled by Corporate Bond Research Project, on file at NBER.

TABLE 33

*Default Rates by Year of Offering, Convertible and
Nonconvertible Bonds, 1900-43*
(percentage of par amount offered)

Year of Offerings	Con- vertibles	Non- convertibles	Year of Offerings	Con- vertibles	Non- convertibles
1900	0.0	35.1	1922	24.7	14.6
1901	8.0	29.6	1923	17.8	11.9
1902	23.8	48.4	1924	0.0	22.6
1903	54.0	29.5	1925	19.6	18.1
1904	59.2	43.2	1926	5.2	22.9
1905	13.4	40.2	1927	35.4	26.8
1906	14.4	45.8	1928	44.1	39.0
1907	20.4	38.1	1929	38.3	30.0
1908	49.8	29.6	1930	52.3	21.9
1909	16.0	36.5	1931	23.4	18.0
1910	4.5	26.0	1932	74.5	12.6
1911	39.9	32.7	1933	0.0	36.8
1912	47.0	28.3	1934	0.0	14.5
1913	39.9	42.8	1935	0.0	6.9
1914	1.6	31.6	1936	0.0	3.0
1915	14.6	26.9	1937	0.0	0.4
1916	16.2	30.5	1938	0.0	0.0
1917	0.0	26.2	1939	0.0	0.5
1918	18.0	27.3	1940	0.0	0.1
1919	15.1	12.2	1941	0.0	1.1
1920	28.7	14.8	1942	0.0	0.0
1921	37.9	11.9	1943	−	1.6

Source: Same as Table 32 for convertibles.

CHART 13

Default Rates for Convertible and Nonconvertible Corporate Bonds and Proportion of New Offerings with Conversion Provisions, by Year of Offering, 1900–43

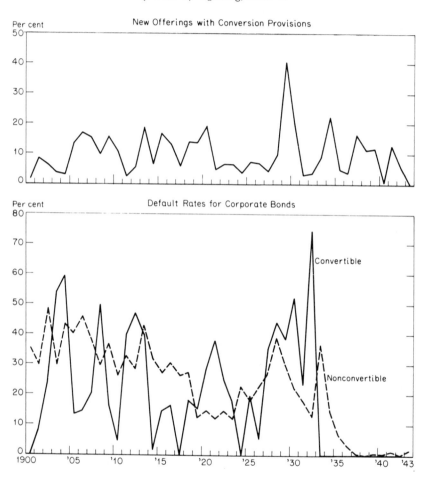

Source: Tables 31 and 33.

TABLE 34

Distribution of Percentage of Dollar Volume of Bond Offerings by Agency Ratings, Convertibles and Nonconvertibles, 1910-39

Year or Period of Offerings	Convertibles				Nonconvertibles			
	I-IV	V-IX	N.R.[a]	Total	I-IV	V-IX	N.R.[a]	Total
1910-19	64.6	13.5	21.9	100.0	46.7	10.7	42.6	100.0
1920-29	70.5	26.9	2.5	100.0	79.4	18.2	2.4	100.0
1930-39	58.1	39.5	2.4	100.0	85.1	10.8	4.1	100.0
1926	83.1	16.9	0.0	100.0	80.3	18.0	1.7	100.0
1927	74.0	22.1	3.8	100.0	82.2	17.4	0.4	100.0
1928	80.0	13.3	6.7	100.0	69.9	27.6	2.6	100.0
1929	72.4	24.1	3.5	100.0	67.5	25.0	7.5	100.0
1930	54.5	44.3	1.2	100.0	91.3	5.8	2.9	100.0

Source: See source for Table 33.
Note: Detail may not add to total because of rounding.

[a]N.R. = not rated.

rating, and lien position prior to World War II will show how accurately these measures operated in predicting default.

Agency ratings of convertible and nonconvertible bonds by year of offering are shown in Table 34. The years 1910–19 are not comparable with the other periods because only railroad bonds were rated in the early years of that period. Nonconvertibles were rated somewhat higher than convertibles in the decade of the twenties, but the individual years did not all show the same pattern. The greatest difference in the treatment of convertibles and nonconvertibles by rating agencies was in the 1930's. Not until 1930 did convertible bonds bear agency ratings markedly below nonconvertible bonds. In 1929, which was a peak year in convertible financing, nonconvertibles and convertibles bore about the same portion of the dollar value in the subinvestment grade (V–IX).

The rating agencies have apparently had as much difficulty with convertibles as investors have had. Table 35 shows default rates for convertibles by agency rating. Except for the twenties, and particularly the last half of that decade, default rates were no worse on subinvestment-grade than on investment-grade convertibles. Convertible bonds

TABLE 35

*Default Rates for Convertible Bonds with
Various Agency Ratings, 1910-39*
(percentage of total amount offered)

Year or Period of Offerings	I-IV	V-IX	Not Rated	Total
1910-19	21.6	21.4	12.7	19.6
1920-29	22.6	45.4	87.7	30.4
1930-39	20.6	14.2	33.6	18.4
1926	0.0	30.8	0.0	5.2
1927	34.5	32.3	71.7	35.4
1928	31.0	94.9	100.0[a]	44.1
1929	23.1	75.3	100.0[a]	38.3
1930	68.5	31.2	100.0[a]	52.3

Source: See source for Table 33.

[a]Based on fewer than five offerings.

not receiving an agency rating were insignificant in the twenties and thirties, but had much poorer default experience than even those marked subinvestment grade. The analysis of convertibles by agency rating suggests that this type of bond was particularly risky in the depression, when the convertibility feature may well have been used to cover up other defects of the security. Convertibility itself was apparently not a mark against a bond when judged by the rating agencies during the 1920's, but in the 1928–29 boom the agencies were able to detect a relatively high volume of faulty convertibles, as is shown by the subsequent default record for subinvestment-grade convertibles.

Market yields on convertible bonds are often not commensurate with the risk of default, and therefore market ratings have little meaning. Table 36 is presented mainly to show the data for the years 1926 through 1930. In 1926 and 1927 no convertible issues were sold to yield less than 1 per cent above the basic yield, but in 1928 and 1929 about two-thirds of them had such low yield differentials. In 1930, the percentage with low yield differentials fell to about half. This suggests that convertibles are likely to be offered in considerable volume in

TABLE 36

*Percentage of Convertible and Nonconvertible Bonds with
Market Ratings of Less Than 1 Per Cent, 1900-39*

Year or Period of Offerings	Convertible Bonds	Nonconvertible Bonds
1900-09	55.1	41.0
1910-19	34.0	35.2
1920-29	31.0	36.8
1930-39	40.9	64.8
1926	0.0	40.0
1927	0.0	55.0
1928	68.8	47.5
1929	64.8	49.6
1930	51.8	66.8

Source: See source for Table 33. Based on par amount of bonds
with market rating.

years of strong stock market action and to be bid up considerably in
value (to have lower yields than if considered strictly as bonds).

In contrast, more nonconvertibles than convertibles yielded less than
1 per cent above the basic yield in 1926, 1927, and again in 1930, when
economic conditions deteriorated. In 1928 and 1929, less nonconvertibles than convertibles had such low yield differentials.

It is hard to generalize about either the level or the trend of earnings
coverage for convertibles (see Table 37). In the first decade of the century, convertibles had a slightly higher earnings coverage than did
nonconvertibles; in the crucial 1920–29 decade, the two groups had
approximately the same coverage. In 1929, the peak of convertible
bond offerings, average coverage of convertibles after taxes was 2.70
as compared with 2.03 for nonconvertible bonds. On the other hand,
earnings coverage was less for convertibles than for nonconvertibles in
1926, 1927, 1928, and 1930. Complicating the analysis prior to 1930 was
the fact that rail bonds were not convertible but almost universally had
poor earnings coverage.

Table 38 shows that, for the first four decades of the century, never
less than 70 per cent of the nonconvertible bond offerings were secured,

TABLE 37

*Average Times-Charges-Earned Coverage After Taxes, Convertible
and Nonconvertible Corporate Bonds, 1900-39*

Year or Period of Offerings	Convertible Bonds	Nonconvertible Bonds
1900-09	1.78	1.48
1910-19	1.74	1.93
1920-29	2.07	2.04
1930-39	1.90	2.86
1926	1.89	2.12
1927	1.51	2.21
1928	1.60	1.94
1929	2.70	2.03
1930	1.92	2.25

Source: See source for Table 33.

TABLE 38

*Percentage of Convertible and Nonconvertible Bonds
Classified as Secured, 1900-39*

Year or Period of Offerings	Convertible Bonds	Nonconvertible Bonds
1900-09	29.4	92.6
1910-19	42.8	84.6
1920-29	21.4	73.3
1930-39	30.4	72.2
1926	49.4	71.8
1927	36.1	71.6
1928	11.4	66.9
1929	15.0	58.4
1930	20.7	56.7

Source: See source for Table 33.
Note: Bonds on which information on security was unavailable
were omitted from the denominator.

whereas less than half and sometimes less than one-fourth of the convertible issues were secured. Interestingly, the proportion of both convertibles and nonconvertibles that were secured began falling in 1926. It began rising again for convertibles in 1929 and for nonconvertibles in 1931.

It is not easy to summarize prewar investment experience with convertible bonds. As a group, they had a poorer default experience than nonconvertible bonds, especially in the twenties and thirties. Defaults among them were particularly high in periods characterized by generally poor default rates and thus, presumably, lax credit standards. On the other hand, the relationship between convertibles and poor quality was scarcely one-for-one; there was some evidence that earnings coverage of convertibles was as good as for nonconvertibles in the first three decades analyzed, as well as in the year of greatest convertible volume, 1929. Seemingly, the convertible feature can be used in two different ways—as a legitimate device for encouraging investors or as an eyecatcher for the speculator to induce sales of what otherwise would be a relatively poor-quality offering. The experience of the prewar decades may provide some insight into which way convertibles were used in the postwar era.

Convertibles in the Postwar Period

The evidence suggests that during the postwar period convertible bonds have been about as popular as in the period 1900–43, if public and direct offerings in both periods are included, or more popular if direct placements are excluded from the postwar data. (The early data do not distinguish between public and direct placements, but the latter accounted for only 7.2 per cent of all offerings in 1900–43 compared with 43.9 per cent in 1944–65.) The postwar peak for proportion of public offerings with conversion provisions (46 per cent) in 1955 was higher than the previous peak in 1929. The dollar volume of convertible issues was well in excess of the amounts in the era Hickman surveyed.

Chart 14 shows the relation between the volume of convertible offerings and stock prices in the postwar period. Rises in the volume of convertible bond offerings tend to coincide with increases in stock prices and fall off at or after declines in the stock market. This is as would be expected for an instrument whose basic appeal is the ability of the owner to change from a creditor to an owner status.

CHART 14

Relation of Volume of Convertible Bond Offerings to Stock Prices, 1944–65

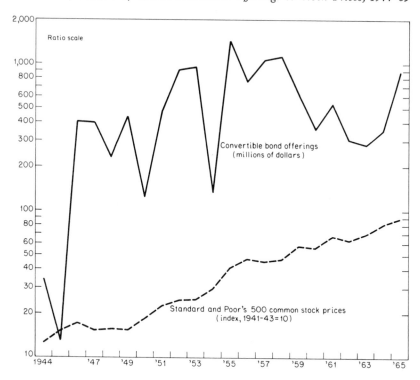

Source: Table F-1 and Standard and Poor's *Security Price Index,* annual average of monthly indexes.

In terms of par amount of public offerings, the proportion of convertibles rose to a peak of 46 per cent in 1955 and then fell to 6 per cent in 1963, but had risen to 21 per cent by 1965. In terms of number of public offerings, the proportion of convertibles rose to a peak in 1959 of 42 per cent and then fell to 28 per cent in 1964. Comparison of the two series shows that the average convertible offering was smaller in the late fifties and early sixties than in the other postwar years.

Table 39 shows the difference in agency ratings between publicly offered issues of convertible and nonconvertible bonds. There was a very modest decrease in the proportion of nonconvertibles which are rated as subinvestment grade from 1944–62, but 1963–65 suggests a rise. There has been a substantial increase in the proportion of convertibles

TABLE 39

Percentage of Straight Convertible and Nonconvertible Public Offerings Rated by The Agencies Below Investment Grade, 1944-65

Year or Period of Offerings	Convertible Bonds	Nonconvertible Bonds	Total Straight Public Offerings
1944	3.8	2.6	2.6
1945	100.0	4.3	4.4
1946	3.2	3.6	3.6
1947	0.0	0.8	0.7
1948	2.9	0.8	1.0
1949	0.7	2.7	2.3
1950	34.1	0.8	2.9
1951	7.3	1.0	2.3
1952	3.0	0.7	1.3
1953	1.7	0.8	1.1
1954	59.0	2.1	4.1
1955	14.9	1.5	7.6
1956	39.1	3.6	10.7
1957	32.7	1.3	7.6
1958	22.2	0.0	4.1
1959	70.3	2.4	14.6
1960	75.3	2.4	7.9
1961	48.9	0.6	5.6
1962	48.3	0.4	3.0
1963	83.7	3.4	8.2
1964	100.0	7.3	16.6
1965	83.2	4.7	21.0
1944-47	2.1	3.0	3.0
1948-51	6.9	1.3	2.1
1952-55	9.5	1.4	3.5
1956-59	36.7	1.5	8.2
1960-63	62.2	1.7	6.1
1964-65	87.2	5.8	19.3

Source: Computed from Tables B-1 and F-2. Based on total rated.

TABLE 40

*Proportion of Par Amount of Straight Public Offerings of Convertible
and Nonconvertible Bonds with Market Rating of
Less Than 1 Per Cent, 1944-65*
(million dollars)

Year of Offerings	Convertible Bonds	Nonconvertible Bonds
1944	94.3	91.5
1945	0.0	91.6
1946	96.3	99.5
1947	99.8	99.0
1948	96.5	95.8
1949	98.5	96.5
1950	92.4	98.2
1951	95.7	93.1
1952	95.9	88.4
1953	93.0	90.4
1954	83.9	92.5
1955	43.4	85.1
1956	52.2	78.7
1957	45.8	37.0
1958	79.5	72.6
1959	76.5	58.1
1960	76.6	92.4
1961	72.1	91.3
1962	73.3	99.7
1963	72.9	99.5
1964	85.5	99.1
1965	87.3	99.0
1944-47	96.4	95.1
1948-51	96.5	96.0
1952-55	73.4	89.7
1956-59	63.0	61.1
1960-63	73.6	95.8
1964-65	86.9	99.1

Source: Compiled from *Moody's Bond Survey*, as described in text.

with subinvestment ratings from the mid-fifties through the end of the series. The net effect of the two movements has been a rise in total low-grade bonds, as measured by agency ratings, from 3 per cent in 1944–47 to 19 per cent in 1964–65.

Table 40 is similar to Table 39 except that it is in terms of high-grade market ratings rather than low-grade agency ratings. The market was less consistent than the agencies; the agencies rated nonconvertibles higher than convertibles in all periods except the first (1944–47), while the market also rated convertibles higher in 1948–51 and 1956–59. At least, they agreed that convertibles were better in 1944–47 and nonconvertibles in 1952–55 and 1960–65.

The Influence of American Telephone Debentures on Convertible Quality Analysis

In the postwar period the American Telephone and Telegraph Company used convertible bonds as a major financing device (see Table 41). In the eight issues offered between 1946 and 1958, $3.9 billion par amount of bonds were created by this firm, or about 36 per cent of all financing by convertibles in the postwar period (1944–65). Because obligations of this firm were highly rated (Aa) and because the com-

TABLE 41

American Telephone and Telegraph Convertibles By Earnings Coverage Before Taxes and Year of Offering, 1946-58

Year of Offerings	Par Amount	Times Charges Earned
1946	343.1	7.8
1947	360.0	9.7
1949	400.0	3.6
1951	365.0	3.8
1952	498.7	4.4
1953	602.5	6.0
1955	637.2	7.0
1958	718.3	5.6

Source: Same as Table 40.
Note: For these years, all A.T.&T. convertibles had an Aa agency rating.

TABLE 42

Median Times-Charges-Earned Ratios Before Taxes, Convertible and Nonconvertible Public Offerings, by Industry Group, 1945-65

	1945-51	1952-58	1959-65
Industrials			
Convertibles	13.7	9.5	4.0
Nonconvertibles	17.8	13.6	10.9
Public Utilities			
Convertibles	5.2	3.9	3.8
Nonconvertibles	5.4	4.6	4.5
Transportation			
Convertibles	a	∠2.0	2.3
Nonconvertibles		5.6	4.8

Source: Special tabulations of data in Table C-1. A.T.&T. convertibles have been omitted (See Table 41).

Note: Ratios were not available for convertible offerings in 1944.

[a]Ratios were available for only one transportation offering in 1945-51.

pany was a unique business enterprise in terms of growth and stability of earnings and general soundness of its operations, the question naturally arises whether removal of the A.T.&T. issues from the analysis would appreciably alter the judgment on quality of convertibles.

As is indicated in Table 42, nonconvertibles had higher earnings coverage in each of the periods into which the postwar is divided and in major industry groups.

Comparison of Table 43 with Table 39 shows that in four of the eight years in which A.T.&T. convertibles were offered, a substantial proportion of convertibles other than A.T.&T. were of subinvestment grade, and this was hidden by the heavy weight of the A.T.&T. convertible issues in the total. No A.T.&T. convertibles were issued in 1960–65. The comparison of times-charges-earned coverage for convertibles including and excluding A.T.&T. shows the latter was higher because it consisted mostly of industrials, which generally have higher earnings coverage (Table 44).

TABLE 43

Proportion of Convertibles, Other Than Those of American Telephone and Telegraph, Rated Below Investment Grade, by Year of A.T.&T. Offering, 1946-58

Year	Per Cent Rated Below Investment Grade
1946	100.0
1947	0.0
1949	11.5
1951	67.7
1952	6.7
1953	4.7
1955	28.6
1958	73.0

Source: Same as for Table F-2.

TABLE 44

Median Times-Charges-Earned Ratios for Convertible Bonds, Excluding and Including A.T.&T. Convertibles, Combination of Eight Years in Which A.T.&T. Offered Convertibles

Industry	Ratio
A.T.&T.	6.0
Other public utilities	4.5
Industrials	9.8
Transportation	2.0[a]
Total including A.T.&T.	6.7
Total excluding A.T.&T.	9.5

Source: Same as for Table 40.
Note: For years included, see Table 41.

[a]Based on three issues.

Significantly, the deterioration in quality of bonds in the postwar period is apparent either including or excluding American Telephone offerings in the tabulation. The reduced use of convertibles as a means of American Telephone financing in recent years, however, has meant that the weakening in quality from early to late postwar years as shown by this measure is less evident with American Telephone omitted than with its offerings included.

In summary, the floating number of bonds convertible into common stock has been a recurrent phenomenon of financing throughout this century. Convertible bonds have been offered in particularly heavy volume in sharply rising stock markets or when financing seemed difficult, particularly for equity funds. Historically, default rates on convertible bonds based on amount in good standing at the beginning of given years have been roughly double those on issues with no conversion privileges. Default rates based on par amount of offerings have been much closer for convertible and nonconvertible bonds because large amounts of the former have been retired (mainly by conversion) before default occurred. The rating agencies had difficulty evaluating convertible bonds before 1944. In the postwar period, by most of our measures, convertible bonds were generally of poorer quality than nonconvertibles. For this reason they have been responsible for some part of the quality weakening observed to have occurred from the early to the late postwar period. But if convertible issues had not been permitted in the postwar period, it is quite likely that many of the same companies would have gone to the straight debt market for funds, which would have lowered the quality of the nonconvertible bonds offered. In general, convertibles as a group were improved in quality by the fact that the American Telephone Company used this means of financing.

APPENDIX TABLES

TABLE A-1

Corporate Bonds and Notes, SEC and NBER Tabulations, 1948-65

(million dollars)

Year of Offering	Publicly Offered Cash Offerings				Directly Placed Cash Offerings			
	SEC Figures				SEC Figures			
	Total	Financial and Real Estate	Total Minus Financial and Real Estate	NBER Figures	Total	Financial and Real Estate	Total Minus Financial and Real Estate	NBER Figures
1948	2,965	13	2,952	2,309	3,008	443	2,565	1,756
1949	2,437	77	2,360	1,936	2,453	400	2,053	1,554
1950	2,360	12	2,348	2,039	2,560	525	2,035	1,692
1951	2,364	63	2,301	1,914	3,326	221	3,105	2,623
1952	3,645	59	3,586	3,102	3,957	307	3,650	2,869
1953	3,856	493	3,363	3,057	3,228	883	2,345	1,942
1954	4,003	184	3,819	3,476	3,484	518	2,966	2,574
1955	4,119	619	3,500	2,929	3,301	748	2,553	2,349
1956	4,225	354	3,871	3,365	3,777	1,011	2,766	2,622
1957	6,118	672	5,446	4,865	3,839	709	3,130	3,108
1958	6,332	287	6,045	5,755	3,320	494	2,826	2,211
1959	3,557	377	3,180	2,926	3,632	972	2,660	2,417
1960	4,806	959	3,847	3,537	3,275	1,063	2,212	2,065
1961	4,700	438	4,262	3,835	4,720	1,131	3,589	3,320
1962	4,440	268	4,172	3,782	4,529	1,164	3,365	3,419
1963	4,714	755	3,959	3,581	6,158	2,056	4,102	4,115
1964	3,623	752	2,871	2,506	7,243	2,639	4,604	4,639
1965	5,570	1,406	4,164	3,821	8,150	2,357	5,793	5,142
Total	73,834	7,788	66,046	58,735	73,960	17,641	56,319	50,417

Source: SEC figures from June 1966 release on Corporate Securities Offered for Cash in the United States. NBER figures compiled from *Moody's Bond Survey* for public offerings and *Investment Dealers' Digest* for direct offerings.

TABLE B-1

Par Amount of Public Offerings of Straight Corporate Bonds Distributed by Moody's Ratings, Annually, 1944-65

(million dollars)

Year of Offering	Investment Grade					Subinvestment Grade				Not Rated	Total
	I	II	III	IV	Total	V	VI	VII-IX	Total		
1944	346.5	355.3	650.0	270.0	1,621.8	42.5	1.1	0.0	43.6	2.6	1,668.0
1945	332.4	1,123.0	900.6	868.1	3,224.1	147.9	2.0	0.0	149.9	15.1	3,389.1
1946	402.3	1,055.3	602.2	436.5	2,496.3	95.7	1.2	0.0	96.9	19.4	2,612.6
1947	320.0	1,492.2	277.6	386.4	2,476.2	16.9	0.0	0.0	16.9	4.2	2,497.3
1948	632.0	863.2	677.8	94.2	2,267.2	16.3	6.0	0.0	22.3	3.1	2,292.6
1949	280.6	959.6	427.6	210.8	1,878.6	43.8	0.0	0.0	43.8	14.0	1,936.4
1950	145.0	691.3	735.5	206.8	1,778.6	56.2	0.0	0.0	56.2	22.4	1,857.2
1951	135.0	937.3	523.6	245.0	1,840.9	38.5	5.8	0.0	44.3	19.8	1,905.0
1952	149.0	1,602.1	987.5	303.0	3,041.6	25.9	15.5	0.0	41.4	7.0	3,090.0
1953	579.0	1,457.1	674.2	288.4	2,998.7	30.1	2.6	0.0	32.7	25.2	3,056.6
1954	409.6	1,259.0	1,156.4	264.9	3,089.9	137.9	5.0	0.0	142.9	17.7	3,250.5
1955	266.0	1,212.7	728.5	476.0	2,683.2	200.3	19.2	0.0	219.5	19.2	2,921.9
1956	645.0	1,098.5	881.3	345.2	2,970.0	322.1	33.5	1.2	356.8	38.5	3,365.3
1957	705.0	1,861.7	1,301.1	599.4	4,467.2	291.5	78.1	0.7	370.3	27.1	4,864.6
1958	888.0	3,027.8	917.2	628.5	5,461.5	201.5	29.2	0.0	230.7	62.9	5,755.1
1959	366.4	1,202.0	654.1	209.4	2,431.9	333.1	81.8	2.0	416.9	76.7	2,925.5
1960	1,063.2	1,203.1	622.5	264.7	3,153.5	143.2	122.5	4.9	270.6	111.7	3,535.8
1961	745.0	1,391.3	827.6	581.5	3,545.4	167.2	45.1	0.0	212.3	74.2	3,831.9
1962	1,138.5	1,175.3	650.7	662.2	3,626.7	72.4	39.7	0.0	112.1	43.1	3,781.9
1963	935.0	1,104.9	731.5	471.0	3,242.4	211.4	79.7	0.0	291.1	27.1	3,560.6
1964	310.0	649.0	719.0	359.0	2,037.0	333.5	68.6	3.3	405.4	61.3	2,503.7
1965	411.0	894.5	1,070.3	603.9	2,979.7	708.2	85.4	0.0	793.6	48.0	3,821.3
Total	11,204.5	26,616.2	16,716.8	8,774.9	63,312.4	3,636.1	722.0	12.1	4,370.2	740.3	68,422.9

Source: Compiled from *Moody's Bond Survey.*

Appendix Tables

TABLE B-2

Par Amount of Public Offerings of Serial Corporate Bonds Distributed by Moody's Ratings, Annually, 1944-65
(million dollars)

Year of Offering	Investment Grade					Sub-Investment Grade V-IX	Not Rated	Total
	I	II	III	IV	Total			
1944	19.5	0.0	7.5	0.0	27.0	0.0	9.9	36.9
1945	0.0	0.0	25.0	0.0	25.0	0.0	0.4	25.4
1946	0.0	19.2	100.0	0.0	119.2	0.0	0.2	119.4
1947	0.0	15.0	10.0	2.5	27.5	0.0	2.3	29.8
1948	0.0	0.0	16.0	0.0	16.0	0.0	0.3	16.3
1949	0.0	0.0	0.0	0.0	0.0	0.0	0.0	0.0
1950	0.0	0.0	82.0	40.0	122.0	0.0	60.0	182.0
1951	0.0	0.0	7.0	2.0	9.0	0.0	0.0	9.0
1952	0.0	0.0	6.0	6.0	12.0	0.0	0.0	12.0
1953	0.0	0.0	0.0	0.0	0.0	0.0	0.0	0.0
1954	0.0	225.0	0.0	0.0	225.0	0.0	0.0	225.0
1955	0.0	0.0	0.0	0.0	0.0	1.8	5.6	7.4
1956	0.0	0.0	0.0	0.0	0.0	0.0	0.0	0.0
1957	0.0	0.0	0.0	0.0	0.0	0.0	0.0	0.0
1958	0.0	0.0	0.0	0.0	0.0	0.0	0.0	0.0
1959	0.0	0.0	0.0	0.0	0.0	0.0	0.8	0.8
1960	0.0	0.0	0.0	0.0	0.0	0.0	1.1	1.1
1961	0.0	0.0	0.0	0.0	0.0	0.0	3.0	3.0
1962	0.0	0.0	0.0	0.0	0.0	0.0	0.0	0.0
1963	0.0	0.0	0.0	20.0	20.0	0.0	0.0	20.0
1964	0.0	0.0	0.0	0.0	0.0	0.0	2.5	2.5
1965	0.0	0.0	0.0	0.0	0.0	0.0	0.0	0.0
Total	19.5	259.2	253.5	70.5	602.7	1.8	86.1	690.6

Source: Same as Table B-1.

TABLE B-3

*Par Amount of Direct Offerings of Corporate Bonds
Distributed by N.A.I.C. Rating, 1944-65*
(million dollars)

Year of Offering	Investment Grade		Subinvestment Grade		No Rating		Total
	Amount	Per Cent	Amount	Per Cent	Amount	Per Cent	
1944	472.8	96.6	–	–	16.6	3.4	489.4
1945	752.1	90.5	–	–	78.7	9.5	830.8
1946	1,038.4	96.3	7.0	0.6	32.9	3.1	1,078.3
1947	1,186.1	98.9	.4	0.1	12.3	1.0	1,198.8
1948	1,736.3	98.9	2.0	0.1	17.6	1.0	1,755.9
1949	1,483.1	95.4	27.3	1.8	43.4	2.8	1,553.8
1950	1,543.2	91.2	7.8	0.5	140.5	8.3	1,691.5
1951	2,512.9	95.8	9.9	0.4	100.1	3.8	2,622.9
1952	2,728.3	95.1	81.0	2.8	59.3	2.1	2,868.6
1953	1,887.2	97.2	10.3	0.5	44.4	2.3	1,941.9
1954	2,394.0	93.0	14.3	0.6	165.4	6.4	2,573.7
1955	2,178.4	92.7	46.9	2.0	124.0	5.3	2,349.3
1956	2,413.1	92.0	6.5	0.2	202.2	7.7	2,621.8
1957	2,564.0	82.5	7.0	0.2	537.3	17.3	3,108.3
1958	2,036.1	92.1	16.8	0.8	157.7	7.1	2,210.6
1959	2,145.6	88.8	22.6	0.9	249.2	10.3	2,417.4
1960	1,900.3	92.0	18.6	0.9	146.2	7.1	2,065.1
1961	3,088.6	93.0	75.0	2.3	156.4	4.7	3,320.0
1962	3,118.6	91.2	85.5	2.5	215.3	6.3	3,419.4
1963	3,720.6	90.4	157.9	3.8	236.5	5.7	4,115.0
1964	4,370.6	94.2	91.7	2.0	176.5	3.8	4,638.8
1965	4,536.5	88.2	160.8	3.1	444.3	8.6	5,141.6
Total	49,806.8	92.2	849.3	1.6	3,356.8	6.2	54,012.9

Source: Compiled from *Investment Dealers' Digest* and N.A.I.C. annual handbooks.

TABLE C-1

Par Amount of Publicly Placed Corporate Bonds Distributed By Times-Charges-Earned Ratio at Offering, Annually, 1944-65

(million dollars)

Year of Offering	1.9 and Under	2.0-2.9	3.0-3.9	4.0-4.9	5.0-5.9	6.0-6.9	7.0-7.9	8.0-8.9	9.0-9.9
1944	154.6	23.7	359.0	240.1	221.5	233.5	308.4	0.0	3.4
1945	66.3	243.1	327.3	269.0	618.1	644.2	127.0	599.4	38.4
1946	0.0	13.8	124.4	303.7	250.9	95.6	534.1	216.5	238.2
1947	18.0	121.0	53.0	261.6	864.8	153.8	15.3	95.8	600.0
1948	15.4	42.0	262.7	369.1	703.7	334.8	219.0	11.0	90.0
1949	52.0	117.9	611.1	367.3	248.0	81.4	69.3	34.0	3.0
1950	41.7	275.0	458.8	472.0	271.6	61.3	83.0	68.8	2.8
1951	0.0	167.4	671.6	417.8	217.5	34.9	75.0	52.0	0.0
1952	77.3	143.8	540.1	835.5	413.8	124.5	256.0	24.0	53.5
1953	10.0	253.7	328.1	555.4	119.8	679.5	123.5	30.0	311.8
1954	20.6	376.0	726.3	598.0	275.5	308.6	329.0	304.0	0.0
1955	7.5	103.5	329.5	493.6	225.0	229.6	637.2	61.5	207.0
1956	102.4	213.4	227.2	605.0	401.7	210.6	291.3	12.4	125.1
1957	38.2	326.3	817.6	928.7	548.8	189.3	411.2	714.9	150.0
1958	79.1	338.5	778.2	636.5	1,540.8	370.4	132.5	362.2	243.2
1959	67.5	302.1	506.6	573.0	289.3	134.0	130.2	364.1	50.5
1960	185.5	296.0	697.8	459.0	397.1	210.0	310.0	172.0	100.0
1961	61.8	621.9	454.2	634.9	276.8	120.5	10.0	320.0	108.3
1962	15.2	805.8	418.4	528.5	295.4	130.2	617.0	265.0	190.0
1963	80.9	348.0	665.5	652.4	322.5	152.0	170.5	362.9	70.0
1964	12.5	629.4	483.0	466.0	183.0	96.3	47.6	230.0	37.0
1965	295.2	564.4	1,245.0	398.8	281.5	180.0	180.0	68.4	195.0
Total	1,401.7	6,326.7	11,085.4	11,065.9	8,967.1	4,775.0	5,077.1	4,368.9	2,817.2

(continued)

TABLE C-1 (concluded)

Year of Offering	10.0-14.9	15.0-19.9	20.0-24.9	25.0-29.9	30.0-39.9	40.0-49.9	50.0 and Over	Information Lacking	Total
1944	28.5	73.0	17.5	9.5	0.0	0.0	0.0	32.2	1,704.9
1945	127.0	134.0	75.0	0.0	6.0	54.5	75.0	10.2	3,414.5
1946	382.4	152.0	55.0	161.5	36.5	50.0	54.2	63.2	2,732.0
1947	190.0	23.5	17.5	55.0	35.0	18.4	0.0	4.4	2,527.1
1948	168.7	6.0	75.0	0.0	0.0	0.0	0.0	11.5	2,308.9
1949	80.1	4.0	220.0	0.0	8.0	40.0	0.0	0.3	1,936.4
1950	167.0	90.9	6.0	0.0	0.0	0.0	0.0	40.3	2,039.2
1951	77.8	65.0	91.0	35.0	0.0	0.0	0.0	9.0	1,914.0
1952	118.0	339.0	75.0	16.0	24.0	0.0	55.0	6.5	3,102.0
1953	227.0	50.0	15.0	25.0	0.0	0.0	300.0	27.8	3,056.6
1954	181.0	85.4	0.0	5.0	15.0	225.0	0.0	26.1	3,475.5
1955	208.0	55.2	266.6	65.0	5.0	0.0	0.0	35.1	2,929.3
1956	579.5	85.2	30.0	155.0	0.2	300.0	0.0	26.3	3,365.3
1957	475.5	187.0	19.7	0.0	0.0	0.0	27.9	29.5	4,864.6
1958	341.6	200.5	15.0	180.0	300.0	150.0	0.0	86.6	5,755.1
1959	287.3	5.0	85.0	0.0	0.0	0.0	0.0	131.7	2,926.3
1960	513.2	24.5	0.0	0.0	0.0	0.0	0.0	171.8	3,536.9
1961	342.1	605.0	145.2	0.0	0.0	0.0	0.0	134.2	3,834.9
1962	400.3	0.0	0.0	0.0	0.0	0.0	0.0	116.1	3,781.9
1963	257.5	375.0	25.0	0.0	30.0	0.0	0.0	68.4	3,580.6
1964	125.0	0.0	0.0	0.0	0.0	0.0	0.0	196.4	2,506.2
1965	162.1	67.0	25.0	0.0	0.0	0.0	0.0	158.9	3,821.3
Total	5,439.6	2,627.2	1,258.5	707.0	459.7	837.9	512.1	1,386.5	69,113.5

Source: Same as Table B-1.
Note: Ratio computed before taxes.

Appendix Tables

TABLE D-1

*Par Amount of All Corporate Bond Offerings Distributed by
Lien Position, 1944-65*

(million dollars)

Year of Offering	Secured Issues	Unsecured Issues	Total
1944	1,789.2	405.1	2,194.3
1945	2,973.5	1,271.8	4,245.3
1946	1,547.4	2,262.9	3,810.3
1947	1,646.3	2,079.6	3,725.9
1948	1,790.3	2,274.5	4,064.8
1949	1,665.2	1,825.0	3,490.2
1950	1,964.7	1,766.0	3,730.7
1951	2,039.1	2,497.8	4,536.9
1952	2,128.4	3,842.2	5,970.6
1953	2,057.1	2,941.4	4,998.5
1954	3,034.3	3,014.9	6,049.2
1955	1,959.6	3,319.0	5,278.6
1956	2,365.6	3,621.5	5,987.1
1957	3,404.0	4,568.9	7,972.9
1958	2,810.0	5,155.7	7,965.7
1959	2,688.2	2,655.5	5,343.7
1960	2,467.6	3,134.4	5,602.0
1961	2,326.9	4,828.0	7,154.9
1962	2,680.9	4,520.4	7,201.3
1963	2,928.9	4,766.7	7,695.6
1964	2,800.8	4,344.2	7,145.0
1965	3,036.2	5,926.7	8,962.9
Total	52,104.2	71,022.2	123,126.4

Source: Compiled from *Moody's Bond Survey* and *Investment Dealers' Digest*. Date on security ascertained from bond titles.

Note: Includes public offerings and direct placements of straight and serial bonds.

TABLE E-1

Par Amount of Public Offerings of Corporate Bonds Distributed by
Market Ratings, Annually, 1944-65
(million dollars)

Year of Offering	High Grade Under 1 per Cent	Low Grade 1 per cent and Over	Not Rated	Total
1944	1,520.3	140.2	44.4	1,704.9
1945	3,087.6	296.5	30.4	3,414.5
1946	2,587.2	24.9	119.9	2,732.0
1947	2,471.5	23.0	32.6	2,527.1
1948	2,198.1	93.5	17.3	2,308.9
1949	1,876.6	59.6	0.2	1,936.4
1950	1,807.8	39.8	191.6	2,039.2
1951	1,782.1	119.6	12.3	1,914.0
1952	2,799.8	289.7	12.5	3,102.0
1953	2,774.0	267.9	14.7	3,056.6
1954	2,991.2	253.3	231.0	3,475.5
1955	1,922.5	992.4	14.4	2,929.3
1956	2,448.1	893.9	23.3	3,365.3
1957	1,880.0	2,977.5	7.1	4,864.6
1958	3,494.1	2,206.1	54.9	5,755.1
1959	1,751.5	1,096.1	78.7	2,926.3
1960	3,180.9	311.4	44.6	3,536.9
1961	3,390.5	411.9	32.5	3,834.9
1962	3,658.6	59.2	64.1	3,781.9
1963	3,497.6	78.3	4.7	3,580.6
1964	2,383.0	60.9	62.3	2,506.2
1965	3,668.1	107.1	46.1	3,821.3
Total	57,171.1	10,802.8	1,139.6	69,113.5

Source: Compiled from *Moody's Bond Survey* and, for market rating, from *Statistical Abstract of the United States*.

Appendix Tables

TABLE F-1

Par Amount of Convertible Bonds Offered, 1944-65
(million dollars)

| Year of Offering | Public Offerings | | Direct Placements | Total |
	Straight	Serial		
1944	31.8	0.4	2.0	34.2
1945	12.6	0.0	0.4	13.0
1946	368.4	0.2	33.3	401.9
1947	389.1	1.5	6.0	396.6
1948	208.5	0.3	21.6	230.4
1949	428.0	0.0	0.4	428.4
1950	122.6	0.0	0.0	122.6
1951	412.0	0.0	60.8	472.8
1952	906.7	0.0	2.2	908.9
1953	943.6	0.0	5.7	949.3
1954	128.4	0.0	5.5	133.9
1955	1,342.6	0.0	69.5	1,412.1
1956	692.8	0.0	64.8	757.6
1957	985.6	0.0	71.1	1,056.7
1958	1,044.7	0.0	70.7	1,115.4
1959	529.8	0.0	88.7	618.5
1960	284.5	0.5	73.5	358.5
1961	452.4	0.0	73.3	525.7
1962	247.3	0.0	54.2	301.5
1963	230.5	0.0	50.4	280.9
1964	282.6	0.0	70.1	352.7
1965	812.7	0.0	76.2	888.9
Total	10,857.2	2.9	900.4	11,760.5

Source: Compiled from *Moody's Bond Survey* and *Investment Dealers' Digest.*

TABLE F-2

Par Amount of Straight Convertible Bonds, Publicly Offered, Distributed by Moody's Rating, Annually, 1944-65

(million dollars)

Year of Offering	Investment Grade				Subinvestment Grade				Not Rated	Total
	II	III	IV	Total	V	VI	VII	Total		
1944	0.0	0.0	30.0	30.0	0.0	1.2	0.0	1.2	0.6	31.8
1945	0.0	0.0	0.0	0.0	2.0	2.0	0.0	4.0	8.6	12.6
1946	343.1	0.0	0.0	343.1	11.5	0.0	0.0	11.5	13.8	368.4
1947	376.7	0.0	11.4	388.1	0.0	0.0	0.0	0.0	1.0	389.1
1948	137.4	63.2	0.0	200.6	0.0	6.0	0.0	6.0	1.9	208.5
1949	405.7	9.8	6.0	421.5	2.8	0.0	0.0	2.8	3.7	428.0
1950	75.6	0.0	5.0	80.6	41.7	0.0	0.0	41.7	0.3	122.6
1951	365.0	0.0	14.2	379.2	27.5	2.2	0.0	29.7	3.1	412.0
1952	654.8	163.7	55.0	873.5	14.4	12.5	0.0	26.9	6.3	906.7
1953	764.5	0.0	156.9	921.4	13.1	2.6	0.0	15.7	6.5	943.6
1954	0.0	43.4	8.0	51.4	68.9	5.0	0.0	73.9	3.1	128.4
1955	637.2	232.5	260.5	1,130.2	179.3	18.0	0.0	197.3	15.1	1,342.6
1956	0.0	265.8	141.8	407.6	228.5	32.5	1.2	262.2	23.0	692.8
1957	35.2	431.5	190.4	657.1	245.9	73.1	0.7	319.7	8.8	985.6
1958	718.3	28.7	56.0	803.0	201.5	27.2	0.0	228.7	13.0	1,044.7
1959	19.9	69.6	62.9	152.4	290.7	67.4	2.0	360.1	17.3	529.8
1960	38.1	0.0	26.2	64.3	94.7	96.5	4.9	196.1	24.1	284.5
1961	0.0	20.3	178.9	199.2	147.2	43.6	0.0	190.8	62.4	452.4
1962	0.0	0.0	105.7	105.7	64.9	33.7	0.0	98.6	43.0	247.3
1963	0.0	0.0	35.0	35.0	118.4	61.2	0.0	179.6	15.9	230.5
1964	0.0	0.0	0.0	0.0	203.5	39.2	3.3	246.0	36.6	282.6
1965	0.0	75.0	56.9	131.9	586.2	65.4	0.0	651.6	29.2	812.7
Total	4,571.5	1,403.5	1,400.8	7,375.8	2,542.7	589.3	12.1	3,144.1	337.3	10,857.2

Source: Compiled from *Moody's Bond Survey.*

Appendix Tables

TABLE G-1

Par Amount of Cash Offerings of Corporate Bonds Classified by Method of Offering, 1944-65

(million dollars)

Year of Offering or Placement	Public Offerings		Direct Placements	Total
	Straight	Serial		
1944	1,668.0	36.9	489.4	2,194.3
1945	3,389.1	25.4	830.8	4,245.3
1946	2,612.6	119.4	1,078.3	3,810.3
1947	2,497.3	29.8	1,198.8	3,725.9
1948	2,292.6	16.3	1,755.9	4,064.8
1949	1,936.4	0.0	1,553.8	3,490.2
1950	1,857.2	182.0	1,691.5	3,730.7
1951	1,905.0	9.0	2,622.9	4,529.9
1952	3,090.0	12.0	2,868.6	5,970.6
1953	3,056.6	0.0	1,941.9	4,998.5
1954	3,250.5	225.0	2,573.7	6,049.2
1955	2,921.9	7.4	2,349.3	5,278.6
1956	3,365.3	0.0	2,621.8	5,987.1
1957	4,864.6	0.0	3,108.3	7,979.9
1958	5,755.1	0.0	2,210.6	7,965.7
1959	2,925.5	0.8	2,417.4	5,343.7
1960	3,535.8	1.1	2,065.1	5,602.0
1961	3,831.9	3.0	3,320.0	7,154.9
1962	3,781.9	0.0	3,419.4	7,201.3
1963	3,560.6	20.0	4,115.0	7,695.6
1964	2,503.7	2.5	4,638.8	7,145.0
1965	3,821.3	0.0	5,141.6	8,962.9
Total	68,422.9	690.6	54,012.9	123,126.4

Source: Tables B-1, B-2, and B-3.
Note: Income bonds and equipment obligations have been excluded.